Abbotsford POPULATION 2310	**Abells Corners** UNINCORPORATED	**Abrams** POPULATION 1904	**Ackerville** UNINCORPORATED	**Ada** UNINCORPORATED	**Adams** POPULATION 1967	**Adams Beach** UNINCORPORATED	**Addison** POPULATION 334
Albion POPULATION 2008	**Aldens Corners** UNINCORPORATED	**Alderley** UNINCORPORATED	**Algoma** POPULATION 3169	**Allen's Grove** UNINCORPORATED	**Allenville** UNINCORPORATED	**Alma** POPULATION 779	**Alma Center** POPULATION 50?
Amherst POPULATION 1037	**Anacker** UNINCORPORATED	**Anderson** POPULATION 412	**Angelo** UNINCORPORATED	**Angus** UNINCORPORATED	**Annaton** UNINCORPORATED	**Anson** POPULATION 2050	**Anston** UNINCORPORATED
Arena POPULATION 831	**Argyle** POPULATION 856	**Arkdale** POPULATION 158	**Arland** POPULATION 754	**Arlington** POPULATION 820	**Armstrong Creek** POPULATION 446	**Armstrong** UNINCORPORATED	**Arnold** UNINCORPORATED
Ashton UNINCORPORATED	**Ashwaubenon** POPULATION 17,160	**Askeaton** UNINCORPORATED	**Astico** UNINCORPORATED	**Athelstane** POPULATION 585	**Athens** POPULATION 1107	**Auburndale** POPULATION 703	**Augusta** POPULATION 156?
Babcock POPULATION 126	**Bagley** POPULATION 379	**Bailey's Harbor** POPULATION 1003	**Baldwin** POPULATION 3984	**Balsam Lake** POPULATION 1005	**Bancroft** POPULATION 535	**Bangor** POPULATION 1473	**Baraboo** POPULATION 12,10?
Belleville POPULATION 2419	**Belmont** POPULATION 985	**Beloit** POPULATION 36,913	**Benton** POPULATION 972	**Berlin** POPULATION 5537	**Berry** POPULATION 1084	**Big Bend** POPULATION 1293	**Birchwood** POPULATION 44?
Blue River POPULATION 433	**Bonduel** POPULATION 1472	**Boscobel** POPULATION 3232	**Boulder Junction** POPULATION 993	**Bowler** POPULATION 300	**Bradley** POPULATION 2656	**Briggsville** POPULATION 415	**Brillion** POPULATION 318?
Buffalo POPULATION 13,575	**Burke** POPULATION 3034	**Burlington** POPULATION 10,463	**Butler** POPULATION 1846	**Butternut** POPULATION 375	**Byron** POPULATION 1648	**Cable** POPULATION 803	**Cadott** POPULATION 144?
Cashton POPULATION 1111	**Cassville** POPULATION 948	**Cataract** POPULATION 186	**Cato** UNINCORPORATED	**Cazenovia** POPULATION 316	**Cecil** POPULATION 567	**Cedarburg** POPULATION 11,436	**Chenequa** POPULATION 59?
Cochrane POPULATION 448	**Colby** POPULATION 1854	**Coleman** POPULATION 723	**Colfax** POPULATION 1161	**Collins** POPULATION 164	**Coloma** POPULATION 452	**Columbus** POPULATION 4997	**Concord** UNINCORPORATED
Cross Plains POPULATION 3603	**Cuba City** POPULATION 2085	**Cudahy** POPULATION 18,359	**Cumberland** POPULATION 2170	**Custer** UNINCORPORATED	**Dalton** POPULATION 206	**Danbury** POPULATION 172	**Darlington** POPULATION 244?
Dodgeville POPULATION 4677	**Dorchester** POPULATION 876	**Dousman** POPULATION 2307	**Downsville** POPULATION 146	**Dresser** POPULATION 893	**Drummond** POPULATION 541	**Durand** POPULATION 1918	**Eagle** POPULATION
Elkhart Lake POPULATION 964	**Elkhorn** POPULATION 10,118	**Ellison Bay** POPULATION 165	**Ellsworth** POPULATION 3281	**Elmhurst** UNINCORPORATED	**Elm Grove** POPULATION 5934	**Elmore** UNINCORPORATED	**Elroy** POPULATION 144?
Ferryville POPULATION 176	**Fifield** POPULATION 926	**Fish Creek** POPULATION 861	**Fitchburg** POPULATION 25,665	**Florence** POPULATION 2319	**Fond du Lac** POPULATION 43,208	**Fontana** POPULATION 1678	**Footville** POPULATION 80?
Frederic POPULATION 1132	**Fredonia** POPULATION 2163	**Fremont** POPULATION 683	**Friendship** POPULATION 720	**Friesland** POPULATION 355	**Galesville** POPULATION 1490	**Gays Mills** POPULATION 494	**Genesee** POPULATION 743?
Glenbeulah POPULATION 461	**Glendale** POPULATION 12,935	**Glenwood City** POPULATION 1251	**Glidden** POPULATION 1380	**Goodman** POPULATION 798	**Gordon** POPULATION 793	**Gotham** POPULATION 191	**Grafton** POPULATION 11,48?
Greenfield POPULATION 36,903	**Greenleaf** POPULATION 607	**Greenville** POPULATION 10,234	**Greenwood** POPULATION 1028	**Hales Corners** POPULATION 7730	**Hammond** POPULATION 1934	**Hancock** POPULATION 419	**Harshaw** UNINCORPORATED
Hiles POPULATION 379	**Hillsboro** POPULATION 1426	**Hillsdale** UNINCORPORATED	**Hixton** POPULATION 435	**Hobart** POPULATION 6254	**Holcombe** POPULATION 1124	**Hollandale** POPULATION 287	**Holmen** POPULATION 908?
Iron River POPULATION 989	**Jackson** POPULATION 6779	**Jacksonport** POPULATION 720	**Janesville** POPULATION 63,479	**Jefferson** POPULATION 7997	**Johnson Creek** POPULATION 2747	**Juda** POPULATION 1097	**Juddville** UNINCORPORATED
Kickapoo POPULATION 566	**Kiel** POPULATION 3720	**Kieler** POPULATION 497	**Kimberly** POPULATION 6508	**Kingston** POPULATION 326	**Kohler** POPULATION 2113	**La Crosse** POPULATION 51,719	**La Farge** POPULATION 75?
Lakewood POPULATION 956	**Lancaster** POPULATION 3868	**Land O'Lakes** POPULATION 927	**Lannon** POPULATION 1109	**Laona** POPULATION 1269	**Lebanon** POPULATION 1632	**Lena** POPULATION 561	**Lisbon** POPULATION 10,0?
Lyndon Station POPULATION 501	**Madge** UNINCORPORATED	**Madison** POPULATION 236,901	**Maiden Rock** POPULATION 118	**Malone** UNINCORPORATED	**Manawa** POPULATION 1377	**Manitowish Waters** POPULATION 642	**Manitowoc** POPULATION 33,5?
Marshfield POPULATION 19,129	**Mason** POPULATION 93	**Mauston** POPULATION 4433	**Mayville** POPULATION 5146	**Mazomanie** POPULATION 1679	**McFarland** POPULATION 7937	**Medford** POPULATION 4321	**Medina** UNINCORPORATED
Merrillan POPULATION 546	**Merrimac** POPULATION 442	**Merton** POPULATION 3353	**Middleton** POPULATION 17,729	**Mikana** UNINCORPORATED	**Millston** POPULATION 160	**Milton** POPULATION 5538	**Milwaukee** POPULATION 597,8?
Montello POPULATION 1498	**Montfort** POPULATION 717	**Monticello** POPULATION 1218	**Montreal** POPULATION 804	**Mosinee** POPULATION 3997	**Mount Horeb** POPULATION 7124	**Mount Morris** POPULATION 1094	**Mountain** POPULATION 89?

Name	Population	Name	Population	Name	Population	Name	Population
Adell	519	Adella Beach	UNINCORPORATED	Advance	UNINCORPORATED	Afton	UNINCORPORATED
Alaska	UNINCORPORATED	Alban	921	Albany	1019	Albertville	UNINCORPORATED
Almon	618	Alpha	UNINCORPORATED	Alto	1096	Altoona	6789
Alverno	UNINCORPORATED	Alvin	UNINCORPORATED	Ambridge	UNINCORPORATED	Amery	2891
Antigo	8156	Anton	UNINCORPORATED	Apollonia	UNINCORPORATED	Apple Creek	UNINCORPORATED
Appleton	73,243	Arbor Vitae	3200	Arcade Acres	UNINCORPORATED	Arcadia	2944
Arnott	UNINCORPORATED	Artesia BeachDells	UNINCORPORATED	Arthur	876	Ashippun	2241
Ashland	8209	Ash Ridge	UNINCORPORATED	Ashford	1847	Ashley	UNINCORPORATED
Auroraville	UNINCORPORATED	Avalon	UNINCORPORATED	Avoca	608	Avon	UNINCORPORATED
Aztalan	UNINCORPORATED	Batavia	UNINCORPORATED	Badger	UNINCORPORATED	Bagley Jct.	UNINCORPORATED
Barneveld	1226	Barron	3425	Barronett	405	Bayfield	490
Bayside	4411	Beaver Dam	16,194	Beetown	734	Belgium	2249
Black Creek	1325	Black Earth	1359	Black River Falls	3403	Blair	1375
Blanchardville	824	Bloomer	3560	Blooming Grove	2322	Blue Mounds	869
Bristol	4924	Brodhead	3296	Brookfield	38,001	Brown Deer	12,061
Bruce	771	Brule	680	Brussels	1112	Buchanan	5827
Caledonia	24,701	Cambria	768	Cambridge	1478	Cameron	1784
Camp Douglas	602	Campbellsport	2025	Carlsville	UNINCORPORATED	Cascade	706
Chetek	2222	Chilton	3974	Chippewa Falls	13,738	Clam Lake	37
Cleveland	1477	Clinton	2154	Clintonville	4635	Cloverland	954
Conover	UNINCORPORATED	Coon Valley	770	Cornell	1475	Cornucopia	125
Cottage Grove	6295	Couderay	88	Crandon	1906	Crivitz	982
Deerbrook	1886	Deerfield	2357	DeForest	9085	Delafield	7100
Delavan	8492	De Pere	24,060	Denmark	2148	Dickeyville	1062
Eagle River	1399	East Troy	4297	Eau Claire	66,623	Eden	880
Edgar	1481	Edgerton	5454	Egg Harbor	201	Elcho	1317
Endeavor	470	Ephraim	288	Evansville	5006	Fairchild	557
Fall Creek	1330	Fall River	1714	Farmington	4154	Fennimore	2496
Fort Atkinson	12,407	Forward	UNINCORPORATED	Foster	101	Fountain City	857
Fox Lake	1517	Fox Point	6734	Franklin	35,620	Franksville	1889
Genesee Depot	UNINCORPORATED	Genoa	255	Genoa City	3052	Germantown	19,823
Gillett	1380	Gills Rock	UNINCORPORATED	Gilman	409	Gleason	2246
Grand Rapids	7357	Grand View	483	Grantsburg	1346	Gratiot	235
Green Bay	105,809	Green Lake	963	Greenbush	2821	Greendale	14,117
Hartford	14,277	Hartland	9136	Hatley	576	Haugen	287
Hayward	2323	Hazel Green	1257	Hazelhurst	1217	Helenville	249
Horicon	3651	Hortonville	2728	Hubertus	5097	Hudson	12,815
Hurley	1541	Hustisford	1122	Iola	1307	Iron Ridge	928
Juneau	2812	Kansasville	UNINCORPORATED	Kaukauna	15,561	Kendall	476
Kenosha	99,738	Kenesha	1262	Kewaskum	4020	Kewaunee	2955
La Pointe	285	La Valle	369	Lac du Flambeau	1969	Ladysmith	3383
Lake Delton	2938	Lake Geneva	7679	Lake Mills	5726	Lake Tomahawk	1110
Livingston	663	Lodi	3054	Lomira	2427	Lone Rock	886
Loyal	1262	Lublin	119	Luck	1114	Luxemburg	2518
Mapleton	UNINCORPORATED	Marathon	1075	Maribel	349	Marinette	10,943
Marion	1267	Markesan	1479	Marquette	150	Marshall	3927
Mellen	730	Melrose	507	Menasha	17,442	Menomonee Falls	35,704
Menomonie	16,301	Mequon	23,178	Mercer	1557	Merrill	9614
Mineral Point	2479	Minocqua	4727	Minong	526	Mishicot	1435
Mondovi	2768	Mole Lake	435	Monona	7658	Monroe	10,841
Mukwonago	7370	Muscoda	1300	Muskego	24,187	Nashotah	1398
Necedah	918	Neenah	25,615	Neillsville	2467	Nekoosa	2582

Badger State of Mind

The Beauty of Wisconsin Through Photos and Stories

Kelly Maddern

madpress
Waukesha, WI

TABLE OF CONTENTS

INTRODUCTION

With Wisconsin being the 23rd largest state in the country - 65,503 square miles, to be exact - it is virtually impossible to cover every beautiful thing Wisconsin has to offer within the covers of this book. Believe me... I tried.

The one thing I can and will do here in this book is share photos and stories from the countless numbers of hours my family and I, along with other contributors, have been lucky enough to spend getting lost within Wisconsin's borders. One of my absolute favorite things to do is hop in the car and drive until I get lost. Considering that the top five most-populated cities of Wisconsin take up only 252 of those 65,503 square miles, that leaves a lot of land to get lost in.

It is just as easy to spend countless hours driving around in a car on Wisconsin roads as it is to kayak, bike, hike, climb, snowmobile, and ski through our lakes, parks, forests and trails. To say which of the four seasons is the most popular is difficult, as it really depends who you talk to. While it's easy to get out and enjoy the awakening of spring, the warmth and activity of summer and the color and coziness of autumn–there is a culture here that also embraces the winter through sports, festivals, food and the holidays.

After spending over two years putting this book together, I had to accept the fact that I was not going to experience even half of what there is to do and see throughout the state before I needed to publish. Fortunately, I thoroughly enjoyed every moment of putting this book together, so I will just have to start working on another book at some point. I met a lot of great people and, along the way, was given the opportunity to blog for Wisconsin Trails. You can find the blog through the book's website: www.badgerstateofmind.com

It has been so fulfilling to create this book, especially since it's something I am quite passionate about. I guess you can say it's part of the "Badger State of Mind."

©Kelly Maddern

WISCONSIN LOVE

Wisconsinites have a lot of pride in their state and all that their state represents. To some, Wisconsin represents the greatest sports teams, strong history and culture. To others, Wisconsin is the farmland their ancestors began to work hundreds of years ago, which has passed through the family and continues to provide food and income. Yet to others, Wisconsin is the place where they can live, work, relax and vacation. Regardless of what Wisconsin is to you, it is something innate and forever. Wherever life brings you, should it be outside our borders, you will always remember Wisconsin and speak of it proudly.

Once a Wisconsinite, always a Wisconsinite.

Something Special from Wisconsin

Badger State of Mind is a proud member of Something Special *from* Wisconsin™. As a book aimed at highlighting the state of Wisconsin's small businesses and beauty off the beaten path, joining Something Special *from* Wisconsin™ felt like an obvious step to take.

What is Something Special *from* Wisconsin™?

Something Special *from* Wisconsin™, a program that has been around since 1983, was created and administered by the Division of Agricultural Development at the Wisconsin Department of Agriculture, Trade and Consumer Protection. The purpose of the program is to clearly identify products and services that are at least 50% produced in Wisconsin. By looking for the Something Special *from* Wisconsin™ logo on your purchases, you know that your money is being spent on a good or service that helps to support our local farmers, communities, food processors, entrepreneurs, and the general Wisconsin way of life.

The SS*f*W™ website, www.somethingspecialwi.com, has a list of current members. The list is helpful for anyone looking for a unique gift, locally grown produce, restaurants, local tourism information, services and much more. These companies benefit from being a member of SS*f*W™ by having the logos and promotional materials, which are highly recognizable, available to them for use on their packaging, brochures, booth signage, etc. Additionally, members receive communications from SS*f*W™ regularly with promotional offers from local TV, radio and print to help advertise their product or service at a discount.

The next time you are at a local apple orchard, in a gift shop or at the farmers' market, keep your eyes open for the Something Special *from* Wisconsin™ logo on products or signage. It will feel good to know you are buying from and supporting Wisconsin businesses.

PROJECT WISCONSIN

365 TOWNS ★ 365 LOGOS

©Project Wisconsin

WHAT is PROJECT WISCONSIN?

Josh Cox, a graphic designer currently working at Kennedy Communications in Madison, wanted to do a daily project of some sort - something that would be fun and a good artistic exercise. In talking over some ideas with his coworker, Doua Vue (a web designer and front-end developer at Kennedy Communications), they decided to join forces for a project. After a few crazy ideas, they finally came up with the idea of doing artwork for Wisconsin towns. They both love the state of Wisconsin, so it was a direction they could both agree on while having fun. And Project Wisconsin was born.

Josh grew up outside of Brodhead and Orfordville, on their family farm his ancestors settled in the early 1800s. He moved to Madison in 2001 to attend MATC for graphic design. He recently moved with his wife to Belleville. Josh's favorite place in Wisconsin is up in the Northwoods; he loves how remote and relaxing it is and would be fine if someone told him that he had to live on the Apostle Islands forever.

Doua grew up in the LaCrosse area and moved to Eau Claire to attend UWEC. He studied graphic design and received a BA in Graphic Design. He currently lives in Madison and has been working with Kennedy since 2008. Doua has really enjoyed the time he has spent on the Mississippi River and up in the bluffs, which provides a beautiful view of LaCrosse.

Originally, the designs for Project Wisconsin were going to be more logo-based. But, after they started, it quickly became more of a branding of towns. They did not have a real method in which they created each logo, just whatever crossed their mind at that moment. Sometimes they based their art on the history of the town or something unique to the town. Sometimes it was based on a pop culture reference that may or may not have ties to that town. Other times, it made no sense at all. Mainly, they tried to not spend more than an hour on each town and hopefully make it somewhat interesting.

The project has become a learning experience for Josh and Doua. They are both interested in history and have enjoyed reading about early settlers, the Black Hawk War, inventions started in Wisconsin and the unique things that each town can claim.

1,200 towns have made it on to the spreadsheet Josh and Doua work from. They scroll through the spreadsheet until something sparks an idea. Although most of the logos don't have a rhyme or reason for the day it is unveiled, some have been coordinated by holiday or humor. For example: Christiana on Easter, Crystal Lake on a Friday the 13th, Freedom on Independence Day, Walker on the big recall day.

The project has gained a lot of attention through social media across the country. People have contacted Josh and Doua to tell them why they should create a logo for their town. Others, who have moved away from Wisconsin, enjoy watching the project for the nostalgia. Project Wisconsin has even caught the attention of celebs such as the 80's hair band, Nelson, who say they always have a great time in Wisconsin. The Wisconsin Senator's office sent an email saying that they loved to keep track of how many towns had logos created that were from their district. They were even contacted by one of the candidates from the 2012 Presidential Election who wanted to use their artwork in their Wisconsin campaign. Although that would have been an honor, Josh and Doua decided against it in an effort to keep their project unbiased in such a politically divided state.

Josh and Doua's project won't necessarily stop at the end of the year. They have ideas of things they can do to continue celebrating Wisconsin, and they hope to have a page-a-day calendar and book for 2013. They currently sell prints, shirts and other items from their website, www. projectwisconsin.com.

HiSTORY . PeOPLe . COMMUNiTY

Long before Wisconsin became a state, the first inhabitants, thousands of years ago, were a variety of Native American tribes. According to wistravel.com, American settlers came to the territory in three waves, starting in the 1820's. The lead mining boom brought the first wave of settlers, the second wave arrived after the Black Hawk War and the third wave was attracted by the farmland. Wisconsin became a state in 1848 and has continued to develop a rich history since.

Many Wisconsinites are very knowledgeable of Wisconsin history and eager to teach others. Each year, hundreds of festivals take place around the state to celebrate history, heritage and community. Museums, libraries, and attractions are abundant, even in the smallest towns. It is not uncommon to sit next to someone at the local coffee shop who is more than willing to share all you wanted to know, and more, about the history of their town or family farm. And each story is quite unique. You will, no doubt, come away having learned something new and interesting.

GREEN COUNTY BARN QUILTS

The concept of barn quilts began with Donna Sue Groves and her wish to honor her mother, Maxine, and her Appalachian heritage by having a painted quilt hung on her barn. With the help of friends and community members, Donna's vision grew to a trail of 20 quilt barns in Adams County, Ohio, which began in 2001.

Donna Sue's idea has resonated with folks across the country and created barn quilt communities in 27 states and in Canada. It is amazing that such a simple idea could have such a huge impact.

Kris Winkler and Lynn Lokken (pictured right) started the project in Green County, Wisconsin. The first quilt was hung in April of 2008, and they now have 120 barn quilts on their official trail. The seed for their Quilt Trail was planted in the Spring of 2007 with an email from a woman involved in a community arts coalition. She traveled back and forth from Omaha and had seen barn quilts in Iowa. Knowing that Kris and Lynn loved quilts, she passed

©Kelly Maddern

the idea on to them. Kris and Lynn were involved in the Green County Fall Farm Technology Show at the time. They did some research and threw the idea around with some professors from the UW Extension. The professors said, "Go for it, it's a great tourism idea." As Lynn left the Farm Technology grounds, after cleaning up from the show, her husband looked at her and said, "so, when do we start barn quilts?" He knew it would happen.

Both Kris and Lynn are members of the Green County (HCE) Home and Community Educators (formerly, Homemakers), who they approached for seed money. The funds were approved and they proceeded with developing their program in Green County over the winter, with the first barn quilts hung in the Spring of 2008.

Because they are both HCE members and 4-H leaders, they were working under the umbrella of the UW Extension program in Green County. With that in mind, they developed a mission statement…

To promote and celebrate the visual arts through the unique barns of the county as symbols of the role they have played in the local economy through the generations-combined with the warmth, beauty and artistic expression of quilts.

The families or groups who choose to have a quilt for their barn, corn crib or other farm building, spend time with the Barn Quilt Committee to come up with a design and the colors that will be used. Each quilt is painted on a pre-built 8'x8' wooden square that is covered in two layers of primer and four coats of paint. Each coat must dry before proceeding to the next coat, so they cannot be built in a day. The fastest they ever finished a quilt was in one week.

To engage the community and tourists, Kris and Lynn act as step-on bus guides for tours around Green County. Bus groups are welcome and tours can be planned, or a self-guided tour is available through the Green County Visitor's Guide. Stops at cheese factories, breweries, Swiss entertainment, museums or for lunch can also be arranged for your bus tour.

Taking a tour with Kris or Lynn is a special treat. These hard-working women are very knowledgeable about everything Green County, including: farming, history and the families that make Green County their home. As they share stories with you about creating each of the Green County barn quilts, they will tell you about their favorites, their challenges, things they may have done differently, and great stories of the community coming together. You can see the pride and love Kris and Lynn have for what they do. For more information about the Green County Barn Quilts, how to get involved or how to have one made for your barn, visit: www.greencountybarnquilts.com.

Each barn quilt in Green County has a story to tell. Kris and Lynn shared some of their favorites:

Probably our most interesting is the "Farmer's Daughter" quilt (#36) on the Bob and Nancy Faith trucking building. Bob worked for Nancy's folks on their farm when he was in high school. After becoming childhood sweethearts, Bob married Nancy... the farmer's daughter.

©Kelly Maddern

Above: The "Apple a Day" quilt is located on the round barn at Ten Eyck Orchard.

Another one of our favorites is "Summer Sunday" (#88). This quilt is on the John & Amy Bartlett barn and has 10 colors of paint. We think the barn is over 100 years old and is used for storage now. John's grandparents owned the barn. His grandmother was born on the North side of the country block, moved to a farm on the East side, married and farmed on the South side of the block and then retired to the West side, where this quilt now hangs. She never left that one country block. We could not find a name for this quilt, so the Bartlett's daughter named it. Sunday is her favorite day of the week for the family in the Summer. The quilt was a real challenge to create. The pattern picture that Amy gave us was about the size of a fingernail, so Kris had to keep looking through a magnifying glass to mark it off. (Kris worked on this one in her garage at home.) It took her 45 minutes to mark one quarter of the quilt, but then once she had the correct measurements it took 15 minutes to mark the other 3/4. All said and done, the quilt looked great on their rustic barn.

©Kelly Maddern

"Grandmother's Pride" (#60) (pictured left) incorporates the birthstone colors of their four children and five grandchildren in the nine diamond shapes.

"School House" (#72) was chosen because both barn owners, Dean and Rea Reeson, are teachers.

©Kelly Maddern

"Maple leaf" (#34) (pictured left) was sponsored by Kim Zettle's uncle, the owner of Maple Leaf cheese factory, which is also where the milk from their cows is sent.

"Swiss Star" (#5) and "Swiss Power" (#104) were specially designed to incorporate the Swiss Flag in the quilt to celebrate their Swiss heritage. Many families in Green County have a Swiss background.

"Queen's Jewels" (#48) was started by the young teen queens from the county Dairy Queen program in honor of Julene, who is the program organizer.

"Grandmother's Fan" (#115) was done as a surprise gift, but entirely by mail and phone. Steve Kraak's farm is in Green County but the gift givers (his mother and 3 daughters) all live in different states. I would talk to his mom on the phone then draw it out on graph paper, send it to her and she would send it to the daughters. The Grandmother Fan design was chosen since his grandmother had made a Grandmothers Fan quilt many years before. We finally got it figured out after several months. The 6 "fan blades" signify the colors from the daughters of their college alma maters UW-Wisconsin (red and white), UW-Milwaukee (yellow and blue) and UW-Marquette (burgundy and gold). They had to get colors that were an exact match to the schools' colors.

©Kelly Maddern

"Amish Rubic's Center" (#46) (pictured left) is identical to a quilt Jeanette Crooks bought at an Amish auction. The barn quilt was painted for Jeanette by her quilting friends while she was battling cancer. Jeanette passed, but the quilt remains hanging in honor and remembrance of her. *(Additional barn quilt photos continue on next page)*

The barn quilt pictured right is the "Tree of Life," which was chosen for this property because it is also home to the "Half-Way Tree." The Half-Way Tree is a large Bur Oak tree that was once used by Native Americans to mark the half-way point between the Mississippi River and Lake Michigan back in the 1800s. The half-way location had been confirmed by the US Survey in 1832, but more recent measurements say it is off by about 6 miles.

This Green County attraction can be found in Spring Grove Township. The road, previously called Old Highway 81, is now named Halfway Tree Road.

GPS Coordinates:
Latitude: 42.583849 Longitude: -89.378322

Wisconsin is home to around 50 Amish settlements and 120 Amish church districts. Within these settlements are approximately 15,000 Amish people spread over several areas of the state. Other than some very small communities scattered throughout the state, the Amish make their homes in Cashton, Hillsboro, the Tomah area, Medford, Green Lake County and Clark County. One of the largest settlements is found near Cashton, where these photos were taken. The Amish sell their goods at farmers' markets or shops, like the ones on the opposite page. The Amish Shop, amongst several other shops, was built in 1994 by the Amish. They sell their handmade furniture, quilts, foods, and books about the Amish lifestyle.

Susie the Duck

©Barbara Anderson

In 1948, a female mallard duck swam into downtown Lodi and laid her eggs in a large rock and masonry basket full of flowers that sat on the edge of Spring Creek. The eggs hatched and drew quite a bit of attention from locals and visitors. Lodi's police chief and his granddaughter, Jean, came to see the chicks and their now famous mother. The chief asked Jean what the mother duck's name should be, and Jean replied "Susie." Susie faithfully returned to her flower basket for years, raising many clutches of eggs and attracting much media attention.

Today, Susie's descendants can be seen swimming around that same basket and other locations in Lodi. There is a small creek-side park where visitors can buy dried corn from vending machines to feed the wild ducks.

Each year, a "Susie the Duck" festival is held in August that includes a parade and a rubber ducky race. Participants pay $5 for one of the thousands of small rubber ducks that are dumped into Spring Creek. The ducks "race" toward a finish line and prizes are awarded based on the order of finish. There are additional activities such as brat stands and beer gardens on Main Street and in Goeres Park.

After returning to Wisconsin in 2000 from a 15-year stint in Seattle, illustrator and commercial artist Barbara Anderson heard about Susie the Duck while working for the Lodi Enterprise newspaper. Barb saw an opportunity to do some drawing, so illustrating Susie the Duck became her first project while back in Wisconsin. The illustrations were used to create cards, which were sold in local stores.

©Barbara Anderson

Barb is currently employed in Waukesha at Perfect Timing, Inc., where she is a product designer. Soon, she will have some of her own designs printed as LANG calendars. A year ago, Barb completed an 11-year-long project to design the book "Crazy Cats Tear Their Skin," which had been written by her late mother, Beverly Hoppmann. The book, a true account of Doris Hoppmann and her eleven children living in Madison during the Depression and World War II, is on sale now.

When Barb is not designing or drawing, she loves to garden and go to flea markets. She enjoys listening to her son's band, Newport Jam, at local clubs and going for walks with her two dogs, Riley and Hobo Jack. When time allows, Barb pulls out the colored pencils and draws new images and caricatures of Susie to adorn items such as magnets, note cards, framed prints and treasure boxes.

Barb and Susie the Duck's home of Lodi is one of three cities in Wisconsin that has its own fair. This free fair, which has been running for 142 years, begins on the first Thursday of July and runs through Sunday. Exhibits include livestock judging, school artwork, baking contests, and local organization display booths. Attractions include carnival rides, games, tractor pulls and the popular demolition derby.

Barb has several other places in Wisconsin where she enjoys to spend time: Indian Lake Dog Park off of highway 19 in Cross Plains, Lake Monona, Lake Mendota, Door County, Lake Nokomis by Tomahawk, and the gorgeous area between Prairie Du Sac and LaValle.

Additional Images by Barbara Anderson

©Barbara Anderson

The Gotten Cabin, built of white oak, can be found just off of Highway 59, on county road N, in Eagle. The sign in front of the cabin reads, "This log cabin was built in the early 1850's by pioneer Henry L. Gotten, a Prussian immigrant. In an attempt to preserve part of the Kettle Moraine history, the log cabin was restored on its original site."

The Grist Mill was built in Hamilton, near Cedarburg, in 1853. Hamilton was the first stagecoach stop between Milwaukee and Green Bay.

The Cedar Creek Winery tour is just one of the activities to enjoy while in historic Cedarburg. The winery is located in a limestone building built in the 1860's along Cedar Creek.

Visit Manitou Island, part of the Apostle Islands, to step back in history at fish camps such as this.

Saylesville, an unincorporated community, is located southwest of Waukesha on County Highway X. Saylesville was one of five independent settlements and trading centers that made up Genesee Township. Settlers began to arrive in Saylesville in 1837, and by 1900, the community had a cemetery, blacksmith shop, mill, cobbler shop, a store with a poolroom in the back, a creamery and the community hall. The Rankin-Booth House, built between 1850 and 1852, is on the National Register of Historical Places.

You can't get much closer to Wisconsin history than at Old World Wisconsin in Eagle. The museum opened in 1976 and features over 60 structures such as farms, villages and outbuildings. Researchers spent a lot of time, prior to building Old World Wisconsin, traveling throughout the state to locate historic buildings. The chosen buildings were taken apart and put back together on the museum grounds. Old World Wisconsin is the world's largest museum dedicated to the history of rural life.

In Spring, when the waters of the Wolf River reach 53 degrees, the Lake Sturgeon travel upstream to spawn. People come from all around to the Wolf River Sturgeon Trail in New London to catch a glimpse of Wisconsin's oldest and largest fish during this annual ritual. Once spawning begins it only lasts a few days, so it is an event with a very small window each year. There are hotlines set up with the latest spawning information or you can subscribe to receive an email notification when the spawning begins.

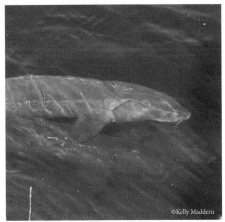
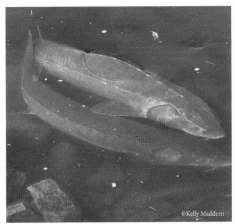

Every year New London holds Wisconsin's largest Saint Patrick's Day Parade. Festivities are held all week, starting with the naughty leprechauns from the Shamrock Club changing the name of the town to New Dublin.

What is now known as "Finnegan's Wake" began as a prank involving a mannequin and a coffin that some kids carried through town, performing an Irish Wake. That was in 1983, and now, about 30 years later, the event has grown to be the largest parade and Irish Fest in the state.

Ashland has been celebrating 4th of July for over 100 years with their popular parade. Ashland, a "great small town to live in," features an early run, parade and some food and entertainment at Lithia Park throughout their 4th of July festivities. The evening concludes with a beautiful firework display.

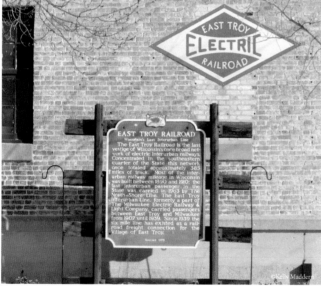

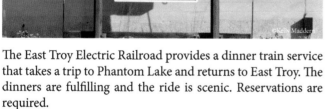

The East Troy Electric Railroad provides a dinner train service that takes a trip to Phantom Lake and returns to East Troy. The dinners are fulfilling and the ride is scenic. Reservations are required.

Fountain City is set between the bluffs and the Mississippi River. As the oldest settlement in Buffalo County, along the scenic Great River Road, Fountain City features the natural attraction, Eagle Bluff, which stands 550 ft. above the Mississippi.

The oldest Dairy Queen in Wisconsin is in Lake Nebagamon, conveniently located right next to the beach.

Um, can you tell me where Buffalo City is?

People fill the streets for Sounds of Summer in Whitefish Bay.

Women Over 90 Project by Kara Counard

There are millions of photographers. Probably thousands right here in Wisconsin. But, just like each photographer has their own style, they also have a unique sense of creativity and a wide variety of subjects that tug on their heart strings. For Kara Counard of Bloom Photography in Green Bay, women aged 90 and older were so intriguing to her that she created a project to collect their stories. Here are the stories of just a couple of the many women Kara spent time with, as she wrote them, including some of the photos she took.

©Kara Counard

Meet Helen...

age 91 and number 4 in the project.

Helen grew up in the Plymouth area. She moved closer to her daughter about 11 years ago, but she still drives back to the same church she's been going to since she was 6 years old (that's 85 years, folks!).

Another really amazing thing is that she went back to school at 33 to become a teacher. Helen taught in a one room school house for five years. She ended up teaching 6th grade in the same school she graduated from in 1938. It was there that Helen taught Language Arts until 1982. She said it was actually one of her worst subjects.

Helen's grandchildren call her "Grandma Fifi" after a dog she once had.

Helen has a 40 year Hummel collection. I've not seen these before. There's even some sort of club. Helen said you have to get the original ones, made in Germany. When you hold them in a certain light, there's a gleam in their eyes.

When I talk about my project, I've been mentioning Helen a lot. She was staying in a nursing home when I photographed her.

Her daughter picked her up and brought her home for the day. She won't have to be there for that much longer, crossing fingers, because Helen mentioned many times how foggy she gets while in the nursing home, specifically in her room. And when she's out, her memory comes back... I thought that was so interesting. And I can't imagine what it's like... She wanted to be home so badly. (and her home is beautiful)

Here's hoping she is home right now.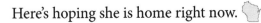

©Kara Counard

Meet Jean...

age 90 and number 29 in the project.

Jean was a city girl. She was born in Chicago. Her father was a furniture refinisher. He owned and rented out the other flats of the building where they lived. Jean said they, the children, were on their own quite a bit. She took care of her brother and sister but would try to sneak away. She said they played in the alley. She also recalled how the toilets were under the sidewalk.

When she was young, her sister died. Jean said, when people died they didn't have undertakers like they have now. They put a basket of flowers on the porch. The color of ribbon showed how old the person was. When her sister died, they had her at a home, and someone stayed with the corpse the whole night. They would also write on the door if there was a quarantine due to illness... "scarlet fever."

Jean also remembered her dad making liquor in the house for his own use, during prohibition. Before the Feds came in, they had to dump it.

©Kara Counard

When Jean was about fifteen, she got her first job at a hospital. She ran an elevator and made up beds. She lived in a building for the employees and went to high school. She took street cars to visit home.

Right after high school, Jean fell in love. She said she got out of school in June and married Adolph in September. They went to the Smoky Mountains for their honeymoon.

Now here's the fun part:
They rented an apartment and bought furniture. And then around that time, her in-laws bought a farm. Jean was a city girl, and Adolph grew up in the city too. But he wanted to be a farmer. So, they moved to Wisconsin. Jean said, about Adolph, "He sure learned fast."

©Kara Counard

©Kara Counard

There was no water in the house. There were no toilets in the house. And they had her killing chickens.

Jean did not have to kill chickens for long. She actually built up, little by little, an egg route. At first, her mother's friends just said to bring eggs when she comes. But it grew. They ended up with a really big route.

And there is a lot of labor involved in the egg business. They cleaned them by hand. Jean's husband did the "candling," looking for spots. Jean would weigh them – small, medium, or large. And they did all of this at night.

They had their egg business until Adolph got his hand caught in the chains of one of the machines on the farm. He lost feeling of his hand. So, in 1970, when Jean was 48 years old, she went back to school. She went to a tech school and learned "key punching." Jean said it would be like data processing now. And she spent thirteen years in that business. I think that just shows her adaptability even more – and her strength.

©Kara Counard

MORE ABOUT KARA COUNARD & BLOOM PHOTOGRAPHY

Besides the Women Over 90 Project, Kara Counard has her photography business, Bloom Photography, which has really only recently become her main gig. Kara says, "I didn't mean to be a photographer."

Kara Counard bought her first camera to take pictures of the clothing that she makes. Then people began to ask her to take their photos and started to pay her for it.

Kara had the privilege of working with a 5th grade class of all girls for the Women Over 90 Project. The kids were able to take photographs and learn about the stories that the photos tell. Kara recalls, "They are so much braver than I am when they photograph."

If you visit Kara's website, www.bloomphotographybykara.com, you will see that, although she is only in her second year, she has really become quite good at what she does.

The Women Over 90 Project recently gained local and national attention through WPR and NPR. See the story here: http://www.npr.org/blogs/participationnation/2012/08/27/160102164/honoring-elders-in-green-bay-wis

The Polar Plunge, a popular Wisconsin event, raises money for the Special Olympics of Wisconsin. Wisconsin Polar Plungers have raised over $10M since 1999. Groups of coworkers, friends or family gather together, some in crazy garb, to take the plunge. The event happens in the dead of winter, when water temps are COLD and the air is FREEZING. This particular event took place in Lake Michigan at McKinley Marina.

Racine is host to "The Big Chill" snow and ice sculpting event each year, 22 years running. The winner of "The Big Chill" snow sculpting competition goes on to the US National Snow Sculpting Competition in Lake Geneva.

Waukesha's 4th of July parade is well-attended and brings participants from as far as Chicago, such as the Futuristics Dance Crew. Kids can participate in the parade by wearing costumes or decorating their wagons and bikes -1st through 3rd place ribbons are awarded.

Memoirs of a 100 year old Wisconsin Resident – Bea Becker

My Childhood

I grew up in Winnebago County, Town of Vinland, about halfway between Neenah and Oshkosh. I was born in the house on the farm, the eldest of 11 children. My grandparents came to Wisconsin in about 1895 from England, then New York State. They came to Wisconsin because of the land that was available.

©Bea Becker

Above: Louis and Lillian Cowling, Bea's parents, married on January 27, 1910.

My mother came from Ashland. My dad's oldest sister married a man from Ashland. After Dad graduated from high school, he went there to take care of the grocery store and the horses owned by his uncle, who owned the grocery store. That is when he met my mother.

School

We walked to school at the Cowling school. It was only about a half-mile away. It was a one-room school for grades one to eight, and nearly all of the kids in the school were cousins of ours. We had outdoor toilets and water out of the pump. When World War I ended, all of the whistles in the area were blowing. We didn't know why. The teacher sent one of my cousins home to see what was happening (he lived in the only house that had a telephone). That's how we knew the war was over.

The teacher had us take the flag down, and the four tallest boys each took one corner. They raised the flag above their heads, and we all walked up and down the road under the flag to celebrate. In the eight years I was at the school, I had five different teachers.

The highlights of the school year were our programs and our picnics. We had box socials and other events to raise money for the school. Shadow sales were big. A woman would dress up and stand behind a sheet with the lights out. The guys would bid on the shadow and pay to have lunch with the person they bid on. At the picnics, all of the parents knew one another. It's different, today, when you don't even really know your next-door neighbor.

We had to go to the nearest town to write our final exams for the eighth grade. Very few boys and girls from the country went on to high school because transportation was so difficult. Today's youngsters couldn't even hope to graduate from eighth grade if they were tested on the same subjects. Maybe they learn more important things now days.

Travel & Vacations

We didn't take many vacations because we were farmers, and the cows needed to be milked. The big vacation place was Keshena Falls, near Shawano. It was a day trip by car. We got a car in 1922. We went to Keshena Falls to pick wild strawberries along the Wolf River.

Through a grange-sponsored farm program, we had three German exchange students. It was during those years that we had our first vacations away from Wisconsin, because the students were available to help with the farming chores. There were places north of where we lived where we could go to pick blackberries. We went to Phillips and stayed in a deer hunting cabin. In these days, there are few public lands where people can go to pick berries. We often took Sunday afternoon drives, such as around Lake Winnebago and in the Waushara County area.

Mom and us kids went once a year by train to Ashland to visit my grandmother. I lived in Ashland with my aunt during my high school freshman year. I was especially interested in the R & R dock in Ashland. They had a smelting place there. Ore was brought there to be smelted. There was a big field that was all full of smelting pots. It was the happiest year of my life. I was accepted among the kids my age. At home in the Town of Vinland and at Neenah High school, those of us kids who were farmers were rejected and made fun of.

Going to Oshkosh or Neenah was a big event when I was a kid. We used to walk two miles to the intersection to get a ride on the trolley that took folks from Neenah to Oshkosh and back. If we went to the trolley stop that was three miles away, there was a store where we could get ice cream while we waited.

County Fair was the third week in September. If we started the school year on Labor Day, we could have Children's Day off to go to the fair. Mostly we ran around at the fair. If we had some money saved up, we spent it on the amusements. We packed a terrific picnic lunch, complete with chicken from the fatted hen that we killed to make our lunch.

©Bea Becker

Above: A photo of Louis Cowling's mother, Bea's grandmother. Specifics unknown.

Holy Hill is a place in Wisconsin where I have always wanted to visit but never had the opportunity.

The Farm

The Chicago Northwestern and the Soo Line rail lines split our farm into two parts. We had to walk more than a quarter mile to get to the other side of the rail lines. When we went, we always took a bucket and picked up the coal that had been lost along the lines. That coal contributed about half of our winter supply of heat. The farmers along the rail line were allotted a certain number of rejected railroad ties. They were made of good hardwood, so in addition to using them for various other uses on the farm, we cut some of them up and burned them in the cookstove for heat. We also picked wild strawberries and wild flowers along the railroad. And we had contests to see who could walk the furthest on the rails without falling off and put pennies on the rails for the trains to flatten as they passed over them.

When I was growing up, Wisconsin had a lot of sawmills and paper mills. Most people were farmers. They worked in the sawmills in the winter time. There were a lot of trees to be cut down. My dad used to tell about how they cut virgin trees. He wept as he told us about how they rolled the trees up in piles and burned them.

In the fields, there were many large rocks—some as large as an automobile. The farmers farmed around those rocks until World War II. After the war, the government had some dynamite left over that you could get, if you had a good reason. My dad got some of that dynamite and blew up the rocks in the field. Some were still so large that you had to use a stone boat to move them with the horses. I had a favorite rock that I liked to sit on when I had a chance to get away. Dad blew that one up, too.

We farmed with horses. In those days, it was a business for someone to go out west to round up wild horses. Then they were trained to be work horses. Once when I was young, my dad went to Beatrice, Nebraska, to buy a team of horses. *(continued...)*

He came home with a team, as well as a Shetland pony, Buddy. Buddy was the main source of entertainment for us kids. We had a carriage, and we drove him everywhere. We also rode him bareback.

Gypsies came every year and camped in tents just down the road from our place. They didn't have horses. Instead, they walked. They swiped eggs from the farm and hired out, if there was work. They were not very dependable workers. We were afraid of them. They mostly just hung around and didn't do much of anything.

CAREER, MARRIAGE & CHILDREN

I attended Oshkosh Teachers' college after high school. I worked for my room and board and got a 2-year teaching license for rural schools. I taught in the Eureka area of Winnebago County. I boarded with one of the school families, and I earned $65 a month to teach 38 kids in Grades 1-8. It was my responsibility to shovel the snow and the coal to keep the fire going to heat the schoolhouse. Married teachers were not allowed in the rural schools in those days, so when I got married, I was replaced at the school. The children in those days were very cooperative. They begged to help out with the duties at the school.

©Bea Becker

Above: A baby photo of Chester Becker, Bea's husband, taken in 1909.

My husband lived on the farm where he grew up with my inlaws. We often took day trips to places like the state capitol in Madison. We also went to Wisconsin Dells. My husband had relatives in Seymour and Phillips, Wisconsin, and we visited those families often. We were very active in the local Grange and continued that membership until the local Grange was dissolved many years later. The Grange was a big part of our social life, and it benefitted the farming community. We were also active in the Wisconsin State Grange and attended the yearly National Grange meeting a couple of times.

I was the local and county 4-H leader in Winnebago county, and my kids were all 4-Hers. As the county leader, one of the things I did was organize the one-act play contest between the various 4-H clubs. Each year, the county's winning play then competed at the Wisconsin State Fair in Milwaukee. My kids enjoyed the State Fair while I was busy with the plays at the theater on the State Fair grounds.

I was also active in Winnebago County homemakers and still am a member of a local club. It was very enlightening for the farmers' wives, most of whom didn't have any education beyond high school. People came from Madison to train our leaders, and the homemakers groups and members were highly respected in those days.

During WWII, I volunteered to help give out rationing stamps for sugar, shoes, flour, gasoline, tires, and other commodities. We saved all of the tin cans that our food came in. The kids enjoyed flattening them, and they were taken to a collection location to be recycled for war materials. We rolled lots of bandages for the war and learned how to make beds with fancy corners so we would be able take care of the wounded if the war came to this country. We had weekly training meetings to learn how to be prepared in case the United States was attacked. There were regular black-out drills.

A group of the women folks who met together rolling bandages, etc., enjoyed each other so much, they formed a group called the Social Neighbors. That group of good friends met for many years following the war.

When the kids were growing up, we often went to Milwaukee to see the Milwaukee Braves play. The county fair was an important time, because the kids had exhibits and gave demonstrations. The Grange had a large indoor food stand, where all of the Grangers took their turn cooking and waiting on the customers. The Grange was also a great part of the kids' lives as they grew up. The Junior Grange met while the adults were meeting, and in addition to having meetings, they were involved with games and crafts. Each year, the local grange hosted a turkey dinner with home-made pies held on the first Sunday in November. That family-style dinner drew folks from far and wide. The adults and kids alike worked that dinner. It was the major fund-raiser to pay the bills for the Grange for the year.

Farming changed a lot during the years we were on the farm. When my husband and I began farming with his dad's help, all of the heavy work was done with horses. My husband was not crazy about the horses, and soon we had a tractor. Then we had another tractor. We had the first self-propelled combine in the area. My husband did the combining for neighbors far and wide.

Sometimes his fields suffered while he did the work for other farmers in the area. Doing that custom work helped pay for his expensive equipment. I had the opportunity to run some of the large machines, and the kids all were involved in the farming as they grew up.

We had chickens—lots of chickens. So we had lots of eggs. This was a big part of our life on the dairy farm. After feeding the chickens, and gathering the eggs, the eggs needed to be cleaned, candled, and packed. We sold eggs at the back door to regular folks who stopped by for fresh eggs. We sold eggs to the grocery stores. And we had two "egg routes." One Thursday we would deliver eggs in Menasha. The next week we would deliver eggs in Neenah. We had a specific route— people were expecting us. Often they weren't home, and we simply entered their houses through the unlocked back doors. We would leave their usual number of dozens—either on the counter or in the refrigerator—whatever they preferred. The egg routes provided the money to put the three kids through college.

Bea Becker celebrated her 100th birthday on August 4, 2012.

©Bea Becker

©Bea Becker

©Bea Becker

Honey
AND
BEESWAX
CANDLES
For
SALE

©Kelly Maddern

©Kelly Maddern

FARMiNG . AGRiCULTURe

Wisconsin, also known as "America's Dairyland," is a top contributor of much of the country's agricultural produce. It leads the nation in cheese production, corn for silage, cranberries, ginseng and snap beans for processing. To paint a better picture for you, that is about one-quarter of the nation's butter and cheese and over half of the nation's cranberries. Wisconsin is also a leading producer of sweet corn for processing, oats, potatoes, maple syrup, cherries and carrots. Did you know that if Green County was a country, it would follow the US and France in cheese production? Very impressive.

The amount of produce that comes from Wisconsin would not be possible without the quality farmland that stretches across the state. Hundreds of thousands of years ago, during the Wisconsin Glacial Stage, glaciers pushed through the state in several episodes. Not only did those glaciers create a beautiful landscape for us to enjoy, but they also contributed to the rich and fertile soils that make up the farmlands.

A Farmer's day is long and tiresome. Their day begins anywhere between 3 am and 6 am, with breakfast around 7am. They are back out on the farm until lunch, and then take care of whatever needs to be done in the office or around the home until the afternoon milkings and feedings. After cleaning up and taking care of everything, it is time for dinner around 7pm. Of course, some nights can be much later.

Eighty-six wind turbines line the horizon to the west of Highway 41 in Dodge and Fond du Lac counties. These wind turbines lend their energy towards the goal of Wisconsin having 10% renewable energy by 2015.

To replenish nutrients to the soil, a farmer may rotate the crops from year to year. For example, a field that grows corn this year may have a different crop next year. The choice of crops to rotate is dependent on the soil and the benefits the crops can lend to one another.

It was once said that farmers are in debt forever, but, although the costs haven't necessarily lessened, farmers, lenders and financial advisors are getting smarter and more creative with maintaining a low debt-to-equity ratio for a farm.

Old farm equipment may become sculptural art when its working life is done. The old, rustic look is hard to reproduce without time and weather. And, frankly, the equipment, like many other things, just aren't made the way they used to be.

Older hay wagons laying around ready to be used.

A hay rake is used to cut, fluff and turn over hay for drying.

First-time farmers who cannot afford to purchase their own land to farm can lease from other farmers to grow their crops. The start-up costs with renting can be as little as $25,000 – depending on what, how much and where you plan to grow.

Old barns are becoming increasingly hard to come by. Their rustic beauty, like that of the old farm equipment, needs time, weather and quality materials to achieve. While some barns are being preserved as best as possible, others are torn down and new barns are put in their place. Fortunately, the wood, nails, doors and windows can be repurposed into something new if it isn't destroyed or burned.

Have you ever wondered why most barns are red? There are a couple theories about why it was the color used centuries ago, before paint. Wealthy farmers may have used blood from slaughtered animals, added to an oil mixture, to create the deep red color. Or perhaps rust, known to be poisonous to the mold and moss that grew on the barn wood, was added to oil, which prevented the wood from decaying. In the mid to late 1800's, as paint was first being produced, red was the least expensive color to purchase, so it continued to prevail as the popular color to paint a barn.

Despite the color of the barn, there were many types and purposes for them. The barns had been built for the type of grain that was housed, the equipment it stored or the livestock it was home to.

Nowadays, you can find barns in almost any shape, for any purpose or in any combination of colors.

7 Mile Creek Ranch - Hobby Farm

Brian and Tanya Hansen left their subdivision lifestyle for a hobby farm, which was something completely new for both of them. They were both from fairly small cities, not from farms, and had no experience with what they were about to get into. For Tanya, having a hobby farm with horses, which is somewhat self-sustaining and that brings in some sort of income, had been a long-time dream. She honestly never thought it would happen. Brian had always wanted to live in the country and have some land to hunt on.

©Kelly Maddern

So, just how did the Hansen's end up with their hobby farm? In January of 2011, Tanya had some pregnancy complications that kept her from working. They decided to downgrade their lifestyle because they couldn't afford the home and lifestyle they had been living. The Hansens noticed an old horse ranch in Lamartine, which happened to be a vacant foreclosure. It was a steal and they couldn't let the opportunity slip by.

Prior to moving, Tanya and Brian spent hundreds of hours doing online research about raising chickens and farming. When they moved in, they had a lot of work ahead of them just to clean up what had been left behind by the old owners. The property had been left to deteriorate, including about a year's worth of horse manure, general garbage, old straw, a couch, lawnmower parts, freezers and more.

©Kelly Maddern

The old barn was in desperate need of work, but Tanya was determined to keep Brian from tearing the top part down. The bottom part of the barn is old horse stalls. Since they knew they wanted chickens from the start, Brian converted one of the horse stalls into a chicken coop with free access to the outside. They were then able to offer cage-free eggs to the public and have enough for themselves.

Brian and Tanya, wanting to raise their five children with an appreciation of the land and raising their own food, have included them in every step of creating the ranch. Justice, their 15 year old daughter, has taken on milking a goat every day. She and the other kids, Noah (13), Kasidee (10), Owen (6) and even little Khale (1.5) are important help on the farm. Some of them even help with butchering the chickens.

For their daughter, Kasidee's, birthday, Brian's cousin bought two Nigerian Dwarf Goats. After some research, Tanya found that they are one of the best milking goat breeds. Their milk is one of the sweetest varieties, contains highest butterfat content and produces excellent cheese, goat milk soap, yogurt and more. Tanya decided that this is a path she wanted to pursue, long term, for their farm. Brian bought one more of the Nigerian Dwarf Goats for Tanya's birthday and then she picked up another buck from championship bloodlines. In spring of 2012 they purchased two more Nigerian Dwarf does of excellent bloodlines and milk producers, as well as bringing in a full-sized LaMancha breed goat to increase milk supply for their baby Khale, as he can only have raw goat milk. All together, they now have five does, two bucks and one wether (their fainting goat, which is a castrated male that can be a companion to either a doe or buck).

©Kelly Maddern

The does and one of the bucks were placed together, in hopes of kids (baby goats) in the spring. That would also mean that milking could take place. Unfortunately, it is not yet legal to sell raw goat milk in Wisconsin. In the meantime, Tanya is researching what she needs to do to start her own business. She hopes to convert an area of the lower barn or the attached pole shed into a licensed kitchen for collecting milk and making cheese. She would then sell all of their products on-site. In addition, she plans to breed their goats and sell some of the babies.

The Hansens are also hoping to produce a lot of their own food. They plan to plant a large garden and sell some of their excess produce on-site. They plan to purchase a steer and a few hogs to raise for butcher. Brian grew up hunting many different types of animals, and he will continue to do so, as it helps to feed the family.

©Kelly Maddern

©Kelly Maddern

They plan to plant a pumpkin patch, and in October they want to have weekend family fun days for locals. They will sell their pumpkins, eggs and produce and would like to offer face painting and animal feedings. Tanya would also love to milk the goats for kids to see.

In addition to everything else, with Tanya's love of horses and the indoor area on their farm, she would love to start a pony party business. They would provide ponies and the space for kids to have a pony party. The kids could ride the ponies, brush them and feed them. Tanya might even expand into providing the food for the parties.

In the winter of 2011, the ranch was incorporated and became 7 Mile Creek Ranch LLC. In the spring of 2012, the Hansens began their venture into homesteading. They planted a 2200 sq. ft. garden, providing them and their animals with food. They raised and sold broiler chickens, and all the butchering and processing was done on their ranch by Brian, Tanya's dad, Greg, and Brian's uncles and cousins. They raised and butchered peking ducks and turkeys for themselves. In addition, they raised two heritage breed Tamworth pigs, one for their own consumption and one that they sold. Two livestock guardian dogs were brought in to help protect their livestock/ranch. Ruby, a Bernese Mountain Dog and Prada, a Great Pyrenese. Tanya began dabbling in making homemade goat cheese, which, she said, is fabulous. Goat milk soap is the plan for next summer. She also did a large amount of canning and freezing with their bounty from the garden.

©Kelly Maddern

At this time, on their ranch they have: goats, livestock guardian dogs, turkeys, ducks, geese, rabbits and over three-dozen egg-laying hens, which give blue, green, white & brown eggs, which they sell, along with duck eggs.

©Kelly Maddern

Another plan in the works is to raise a pig for an annual community pig roast on the ranch each fall.

If you wish to reach the ranch, please contact them at
www.freewebs.com/7milecreekranch
or on Facebook under 7 Mile Creek Ranch LLC.

The best time to plant corn in Wisconsin is around May 1st in the southern half of the state and May 7th in the northern half.

Corn growth is dependent on soil type, water and nutrients, and any sort of disease. Typical field corn for grain can grow to a height of 6-9 feet. Other corn varieties can grow up to 10-15 feet.

"Knee High by Fourth of July"... That used to be the old adage for the crop. Now, if the crop is that tall at the 4th of July, it's behind.

Before tractors, farmers used oxen. They are the ultimate machine for a small farm because they only eat grass, can work for up to 14 years, provide fertilizer and can be eaten when they die.

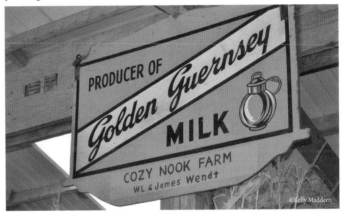

There are six main breeds of cows in Wisconsin. Ayrshires are red and white and are considered an outstanding commercial dairy cattle. The Brown Swiss cows adapt well to their climate and produce large quantities of milk, which is great for making cheese. The Guernsey cow is known for their high-butterfat and high-protein milk. Holsteins are recognizable by their red and white or black and white (*cont.*)

patterns. They are outstanding milk producers. The Jersey cow are a smaller breed with great milk production. Because they are small, their maintenance costs are less for the amount of milk that they produce. The Milking Shorthorn is one of the oldest breeds in the world. They are red, white, or a mix of red and white. They are able to produce for a long time, which makes them a valuable cow.

Traditionally, horses were used to haul heavy loads, transport people and plow the fields. Today, horses are still used to herd sheep and cattle, and they help police patrol during festivals and other venues where other transportation may not work well. Horses today are used more often for riding and competition.

In Wisconsin, we are fortunate to have many horse-friendly trails and campgrounds. The trails range from easy to difficult and can be found throughout the state. Some campgrounds are designed to accommodate horseback riders with a place to keep your horse, riding arenas and trails. Some trails connect to state trails outside the campground.

There are many llama farms around the state of Wisconsin. Llamas are preferred by some to raise because of their gentle nature, they are easy to teach, they eat diverse amounts of food and they produce a soft wool.

Goats and sheep can be found on many farms throughout Wisconsin. Goat milk is not only a popular milk used when dairy milk is not tolerated, it is also used to make materials such as soap, cheeses, yogurt, butter and much more.

Sheep provide wool, cheese, yogurt, butter, ice cream, and, along with goats, are great at managing the landscape.

Every year the state hosts the Wisconsin Sheep and Wool Festival at the beginning of September. The festival features classes, youth activities, stock dog trials, auctions and sales, clinics, and much more.

Harvest time is a special time in Wisconsin. The trees turn brilliant colors, the people bundle in clothing they haven't worn in several months, and farms invite the community to see and purchase their crop of pumpkins, apples and squashes. The farms feature activities such as hay rides, caramel apple booths, corn mazes, pony rides, and food tents. Crafts created from Indian Corn, pumpkins or squash are usually for sale. It's a cozy and magical time in Wisconsin, all in preparation for Halloween and Thanksgiving.

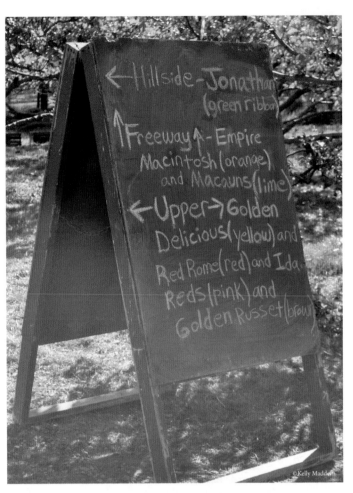

RECReaTiON

When Wisconsinites say that they love Wisconsin, it's probably not because of all the cows, farms and corn... although cows are pretty cool, farms are fun to visit and corn is quite tasty. People love Wisconsin because there are so many things to do and see that you may not get many other places. Wisconsin is a nice package of everything... in a pretty, water-bordered package.

Within those borders (Lake Superior, Lake Michigan and the Mississippi River) are thousands of lakes, miles of trails, acres of forest, hundreds of cities and all sorts of fun. In fact, there is so much fun to be had, you may not be able to accomplish it all in a lifetime. Challenge... On!

You don't have to be an outdoor enthusiast to enjoy Wisconsin – just ask anyone who lives here year-round and hates winter. The four seasons bring the hottest temps to the coldest temps, as well as all of the beautiful weather in between. Let Wisconsinsites show you how you can spend each and every day in any type of weather.

Anchored rafts in the lake are fun to swim to, and even more fun to jump off of.

Or just take a run off the pier and jump right in.

With so many lakes in Wisconsin, many families have a cabin or cottage they can retreat to. It's great to spend a weekend on the lake.

Whether you are a serious fisherman or a first-timer, you can feel comfortable casting a line in Wisconsin waters.

Lake Michigan is Wisconsin's ocean... without the saltwater.

If you are more comfortable on the smaller lakes, there are plenty, such as the beautiful Okauchee Lake in Lake Country.

Lake Geneva is a beautiful place to bring your boat or grab a rental. There is something for everyone in this resort town.

Tie up your boat and go ashore for some lake side dining in one of Wisconsin's lake towns. Many lake side restaurants and bars are accessible by boat...

... or if you prefer, tie your boat up to an island in the middle of the lake, like here in Chetek, and bring your own picnic and drinks.

Many lakes throughout Wisconsin have public beaches, with or without lifeguards.

Grab your water skis or wakeboard for a fun ride through the water.

If you prefer to sit, a wave runner might be more your thing.

If you want a more leisurely ride, kayaks are the perfect way to take in the beauty of the lakes.

If you find yourself at Frame Park in Waukesha, you have a choice of several types of boats.

Paddle boats are a fun choice for a family or group of four.

Canoes are another option for a few people to explore Wisconsin's waters. Grab a waterproof bag to bring your camera along.

Paddle boarding, which began in 1930, has been gaining in popularity. This guy is paddling the calm waters of Lake Superior.

Saxon Harbor, in far northern Wisconsin along Lake Superior, has a beautiful beach tucked away from the main roads.

Little Sand Bay, one of the northern-most points of mainland Wisconsin, is part of the Apostle Islands National Lakeshore. At Little Sand Bay, you can camp, swim at the beach, explore some trails or kayak. The beach is worth exploring, as you will find unique, secluded areas.

You may be surprised by how far you can walk out into Lake Superior and still be in ankle or knee-high water. You will be thankful for the extra time to get used to the cold water.

The Lake Superior coastline and the Apostle Islands are very popular places to kayak and explore the Northwoods beauty.

Lake Superior is like swimming in an infinity pool - nothing but the blue horizon.

Hannah Mast - Log Roller

©Hannah Mast

Wisconsin's logging history dates back to the 19th century, when lumber was in demand for building the growing cities across the United States. The Northwoods provided a large amount of lumber and generated much needed jobs. For many lumberjacks, their job became a source of recreation and competition.

Log rolling, also known as birling, is a sport that began when the logs were sent down the river and would become jammed. The lumberjacks would have to dislodge the jam, hopefully without getting hurt in the process. To successfully take care of the jams, the lumberjacks learned to balance on the logs. At the end of the trip down river, the lumberjacks, also known as river pigs or log drivers, would compete against the other lumberjacks for the title of best birler.

©Hannah Mast

©Hannah Mast

©Hannah Mast

In 1926, Washburn, Wisconsin became the home to the International Log Rolling Association. The group was organized to put competition rules in place for the World Log Rolling Championships.

Today, log rolling is taught through city recreation departments, at camps, and even through local YMCAs. The Wisconsin logging history lives on through organizations such as Madison Log Rolling, LLP, which opened in 2010 and teaches the balance and agility you need to be a successful log roller.

Hannah Mast, an 18-year-old instructor at Madison Log Rolling, grew up in Hayward and has been log rolling since she was two years old. Although Hannah was too young to take lessons at the Lumberjack Bowl, where the Lumberjack World Championships are held in Hayward, a gentleman named JR Salzman took her under his wing and gave her lessons at his house.

As Hannah grew up, she always took to sports very easily, as did her best friend Meredith Ingbretson. They both log rolled together for as long as they can remember, and they usually held some of the top rankings through the amateur levels. Hannah won many first place awards, including the ILRA World Rolling Championships in 2005 in the U10 girls division.

Hannah's siblings, Nick and Andrea Mast, have both competed at the professional level. Since Hannah made the jump to the professional level, she has not won any competitions and is working hard to earn her place. She has made a lot of talented, kind, and family-like friends along the way, which has become one of her biggest rewards. Amongst all of the sports she competes in, log rolling has shown her the greatest sense of family amongst competitors.

Hannah moved from Hayward in the fall of 2008 because she was offered a spot on the Madison Capitol's Girls AAA hockey team. Hockey has been her main sport and she was nervous, yet excited, to take a chance with this opportunity. Hannah hopes to develop into a D1 or D3 college hockey goaltender.

Hannah's mom moved to Waunakee with her, while her dad remained in Hayward to keep their family business, Mast Construction, running. She says she cannot thank her parents enough for taking on the challenge of living in separate towns in order for her to play on the hockey team. Hannah and her mother make their way back to Hayward as much as possible and usually spend the entire summer there. Hannah says that she will always make it back to Hayward for the Lumberjack Championships and plans to never miss a single one.

This has been Hannah's first year working with Madison Log Rolling. For Hannah, it has been a huge privilege to be able to teach for Shana Martin. Shana Martin does a lot of work with Huntington's Disease Society of America (HDSA), which has been a big inspiration for Hannah and others.

From here, Hannah hopes to continue log rolling, keep the tradition alive and continue to make lifelong friends. She plans to attend college, possibly for psychology. Regardless of where she ends up, she will always remember her Hayward roots and always consider it home.

©Hannah Mast

©Hannah Mast

©Hannah Mast

©Hannah Mast

©Hannah Mast

This is the perfect way to enjoy the beach, even if you don't want to get in the water.

Fox Brook Park in Brookfield offers sectioned-off swimming areas for the least experienced to the more advanced.

There is nothing like taking the kayak out on the lake first thing in the morning. The photo ops are great, the air is refreshing and it is the most peaceful time to be alone with your thoughts.

While out on the water, it's fun to check out everyone else's lakeside property and water toys. Stop in at Eagle Spring Pub in Eagle to "Canoe to Lulu." Canoe and paddle boat rentals are available right from the restaurant, across the road from Eagle Spring Lake.

The lakes aren't just for people... there are many parks that allow dog access, including Buckhorn State Park in Necedah.

Pewaukee Lake has one of the most accessible beaches, with their downtown right across the street.

Before heading to a Moonlit Movie at Fowler Park in Oconomowoc, take a seat along the lake and watch the Badgerland Ski Show. Food is available at food tents in the park, and the lakeshore provides plenty of seating.

After the Ski Show, be sure to get back down to the movie grounds for a great view of the night's feature movie.

©Kelly Maddern

©Kelly Maddern

©Kelly Maddern

©Kelly Maddern

Bayfield is one of Wisconsin's northern-most populated cities. The town is the gateway to the Apostle Islands, as well as being its own unique destination. In Bayfield, you can visit orchards, enjoy Apple Festival, spend some time shopping or enjoy a fish boil. If you want to head out on the water and away from town, you can take the ferry to Madeline Island, take the Apostle Island Cruise or sail the day away in a sailboat.

The carved and sculpted Wisconsin landscape is very attractive to thrill-seekers. Cliff-jumping is fun and exciting for those who are familiar with the waters below.

If you are a little less adventurous, there are many other ways to enjoy the waters of Wisconsin.

Chetek, otherwise known as the "City of Lakes" and the home of Fish-o-Rama, sits along a chain of six lakes: Chetek Lake, Prairie Lake, Pokegama Lake, Ojaski Lake, Ten Mile Lake and Moose Ear Lake. By boat, you can access restaurants, bars, resorts and campgrounds.

Within the chain of lakes are islands – some with houses, some that are owned (like this one), and others that are not.

Pontoon boats are popular on the chain of lakes. When you pass by another boat, you can expect friendly hand waves.

Along the island shores you can drop your anchor and enjoy swimming at the sand bars. If you pay attention to the depth finder on your boat, you will find other sand bars throughout the lakes to stop at.

The Chetek area is just as enjoyable for kids as it is for adults. There is plenty to do, whether you come with family or friends.

©Kelly Maddern

Wisconsin is a kayaker's paradise, regardless of the type of kayaker you are. There are small lakes, large lakes, small rivers and large rivers – and everything in between. Door County, the Apostle Islands and places like the St. Croix River (above) are kayaker playgrounds.

Kayakers looking for rapids can find them throughout the state. The Wolf River is one of the fastest-flowing rivers, as it drops 430 feet over 28 miles.

Many of Wisconsin's lakes and rivers are fairly calm and enjoyable for kayakers looking for a more leisurely trip.

Wisconsin Couple Publishes Magazine About Pilots, Planes & Places

Dave and Peggy Weiman founded *Wisconsin Flyer* magazine in 1978 from the basement of their home in Oregon, Wisconsin with $5,000 Peggy had saved to buy their first airplane. Within a year, the Weimans generated enough revenue from advertising and subscription sales that they were able to pay back their initial investment and bought their first airplane – a 1946 Cessna 140 – a little two-seat airplane that cruised at 95 mph.

During the first few years both Dave and Peggy continued to work for the University of Wisconsin while they published the magazine at night and on weekends. Dave left the University in 1981 to work full time publishing the magazine, which had expanded to cover the Midwest and was renamed "Midwest Flyer Magazine" in 1980. Peggy continued to work at the university, began raising two children, and after about 10 years, joined Dave full time publishing the magazine.

The magazine grew from covering only Wisconsin to 11 Midwest states including Wisconsin, Minnesota, North Dakota, South Dakota, Iowa, Nebraska, Kansas, Missouri, Illinois, Indiana, and Michigan. In 2011, the magazine expanded to also include Ohio because of the state's rich aviation history.

Midwest Flyer Magazine has grown from 12 black and white pages in 1978 to 64 color pages today — more than five times its original size – and circulation has likewise increased!

Photo by Joseph W. Jackson III

The magazine is for and about aircraft owners and pilots, airport managers and engineers, corporate flight department managers and pilots, flight center operators, aircraft maintenance technicians, flight instructors, aviation educators, and aviation support service professionals.

Dave Weiman is editor and director of advertising. He holds degrees from Metropolitan State College-Minneapolis (ALA), the University of Minnesota- Minneapolis (BA), and the University of Wisconsin- Madison (MS). Dave was on the faculty at the University of Wisconsin in extension education prior to publishing *Midwest Flyer Magazine*. He started flying in 1971 and holds a Private Pilot Certificate (Land & Sea), an Instrument Rating, and High Altitude, Complex Gear, and Tailwheel endorsements. Dave and Peggy Weiman have owned three aircraft and currently own a 1976 Cessna 182 Skylane painted in its original bicentennial red, white and blue colors.

Peggy Weiman is director of production, circulation, and electronic media. She holds a degree from Granite Falls Technical College in Minnesota, and has received advanced training in computer science and graphic design. Priorto publishing *Midwest Flyer Magazine*, Peggy held administrative positions at the University of Wisconsin-Madison campus.

Midwest Flyer Magazine has 29 contributing writers and photographers who share the Weimans' passion for flight. It is this combined effort, which has made *Midwest Flyer Magazine* an award-winning publication, both in print and online (www.MidwestFlyer.com).

Readers regularly comment: "The current issue is better than the last," which is evident in the awards bestowed *Midwest Flyer Magazine*:

"National Journalism Award" for superior news coverage of aviation issues nationwide (National Association of State Aviation Officials, 2010).

"AOPA Presidential Citation" for 25 years of quality aviation reporting (Aircraft Owners & Pilots Association, 2003).

"Aviation Business of the Year Award" (Wisconsin Aviation Trades Association, 2000 and 2009).

"Award of Excellence" for outstanding leadership and the promotion of aviation in the state of Minnesota (Minnesota Council of Airports, 2004).

"Blue Light Award" for excellence in reporting aviation news and information (Wisconsin Airport Management Association, 1981 & 2005).

From hard-hitting editorials and columns from experts in aviation law, pilot health, flight training, aircraft maintenance, and airport development, to feature stories about pilots, planes, airport restaurants and travel destinations, and the most complete and current calendar of aviation events in the Midwest, *Midwest Flyer Magazine* has the content readers are looking for without all of the fluff! People may skim over other aviation publications, but they read *Midwest Flyer Magazine* from cover to cover.

It's a beautiful sight to have a random hot air balloon fly right over your house. There are several hot air balloon festivals in Wisconsin throughout the year: Hudson's Hot Air Affair, Waterford's Hot Air Balloon Festival and Wausau's Balloon Rally and Glow.

Did you know that Wisconsin ranks third in the country (according to The League of American Bicyclists) for the number of miles of scenic on-and-off-road trails and paths?

Alpine Valley Music Theater is a popular outdoor music venue where half the fun is spending the day tailgating in the parking lot before the show. Concert-goers bring grills, tents, games, foods, beverages and music to have hours of pre-show fun around their cars.

Alpine Valley is located in East Troy, which is conveniently located between Madison, Milwaukee, Rockford and Chicago. The venue was built in 1977 and has hosted many popular acts over the years who consider the theater to be their favorite place to play in the country.

Camping is a very popular activity in Wisconsin. There are many private campgrounds, as well as sites located within the state parks. There are campgrounds to suit everyone's camping style, whether you are hiking in with a backpack or bringing a large camper.

Most campsites provide a campfire ring and picnic table. Electricity, water and flush toilets are dependent on the campground and site you choose.

With an abundant amount of lakes and rivers in Wisconsin, many of the campgrounds are set along a of body of water.

There are many picturesque golf courses throughout the state. GolfWisconsin.com is a great resource to find a course to play, including a list ranking the best in Wisconsin.

Bay Beach Wildlife Sanctuary and Amusement Park are located in Green Bay. The amusement park has been around since 1892 and has maintained very low costs for the rides, currently at 25¢ per ticket, 1-2 tickets per ride. The sanctuary is an urban refuge set on 700 beautiful acres and is home to more than 4,500 orphaned or injured animals.

Wisconsin certainly does not lack in the amount of fairs and festivals held throughout the year. There are celebrations which honor community, culture, history, food, beverages, city mascots, music, legends and much more. Visit wisconsinfairsandfestivals.com for a large list.

The entertainment at each fair or festival varies greatly, depending on the event. If you go to a wine festival at a local winery, you can expect to watch grape stomping contests, taste testing and music. If you go to a county fair, you will see rides, animals, music and lots of food.

Each October during Ducktoberfest at the Duckpond (Madison Mallards ball park), Dachshunds race to become the top "wiener."

At the Delafield Block party in July, you can enjoy food from the local restaurants, music and watch events like this wakeboard competition.

Wisconsin has a great crop of local musicians to enjoy at the fests. The Whiskey Belles, from Milwaukee, are an excellent example of a local band with a great following. Their mix of country, folk and Americana is a very popular sound at festivals around the state.

Mama Digdown's Brass Band

Mama Digdown's Brass Band is a local New Orleans style brass band that incorporates jazz, funk, rock and hip hop into their tunes. Christopher (Roc) Ohly and Erik Jacobson met in Madison at the UW School of Music, and started the band in 1993 by trying to find other guys that wanted to play this kind of music. They once auditioned a trombone player at a party and the guy played with them for 5 years.

"Mama Digdown is the woman who adopted all of us pick-pocketing orphans (like Oliver) and paid for band lessons. When she died, we started the band to play at her funeral. It was our first gig," Erik shared in regards to how they came up with the name of the band.

©Kelly Maddern

The band started going down to New Orleans more than 15 years ago. Four of the band members jumped into the band van after a gig in Madison one night. They drove straight through and found themselves at Donna's Bar listening to the New Birth Brass Band. From then, they were hooked. They gave Donna, the owner of Donna's Bar, a copy of their CD and she put it in her juke box. Next time they went down to New Orleans, she said people loved it and she wanted to hire them.

Besides having played in New Orleans around fifty times and throughout Wisconsin, they have played in Europe three times and every corner of the US. The types of events have included weddings, funerals, lavish parties, jazz festivals, house parties, parades, club gigs, beer festivals and everything else in between.

©Mama Digdown's Brass Band

Erik explained more about their connection with New Orleans, "With very few exceptions, brass band musicians in New Orleans are black and the brass band tradition itself is one of the black community. When we first started playing in New Orleans, the brass band musicians were a bit amused but also very interested in the fact that we were playing their music. As a band we have always been so deferential and respectful of the tradition, and I think that is felt by the musicians and fans there. We take the music very seriously and I think the other bands are flattered that we are so interested in their music. The crowds, too, have always gotten a kick out of "the white boys from Wisconsin," but they know we are serious and treat us accordingly. At this point, many assume we are, in fact, from New Orleans. After Branford Marsalis heard us at a show one night and then found out we were from Madison, he had a puzzled look on his face and said 'I thought ya'll was from back home.' Even though we are outsiders, we have been embraced by the brass band community.

"One of our trumpet players, Jeff Maddern, took some time off from Mama Digdown's and lived in New Orleans. He was a member of the Hot 8 Brass Band while he was there. He also played second line parades and club gigs with New Birth and the Lil' Rascals. Some New Orleans bands have played a couple of our original songs. Rebirth, Hot 8 and The

Stooges have all played songs penned by members of Mama Digdown's. We have built friendships with many of the bands of New Orleans. On several occasions we have had brass bands come up north to play some shows.

"When Katrina hit, many of us were in contact with our friends in New Orleans. We all felt so sad. When we found out that so many musicians had lost their instruments, we decided to start an instrument drive. In the end we collected about 60 horns and drums and my dad and I drove them down (to New Orleans) and the Tipitina's Foundation gave them to musicians that needed them. We also booked the Stooges Brass Band into about 15 clubs right after the storm. In all, I think we raised about $7,000 to help out musicians, but that really is nothing compared to the level of need at the time."

Each of Mama Digdown's members contributes their ideas to help choose what they are going to play. One of them might hear a song on the radio and present it to the band as something they'd like to try out. Other band members have written a lot of originals for them to play.

"If you're loyal, a badass and a true Digdown brother, you get a letter jacket. It takes a while to earn your jacket though. You need to be there through thick and thin. Some guys have them, some are getting close. It's like the green jacket in the Masters," Erik explained.

As with any band, Digdown has had their share of challenges. Right now, the biggest challenge is that they live in four different cities – Madison, Chicago, Milwaukee and Minneapolis. It takes a lot of planning and preparation to get the eight musicians from four cities together to perform.

Despite the challenges they've had, they have had some big successes. For three summers, the band was asked to play at a jazz festival in Ascona, Switzerland. Ascona is a small village in the southern part of Switzerland, right on the border with Italy. Erik says it's the most beautiful place he has been to. Ascona is right on Lake Maggiore in the mountains. Each summer they have a 12-day jazz festival that is geared towards New Orleans music. Mama Digdown's recorded a Live from Ascona album while they were there.

©Kelly Maddern

Digdown has put out 9 albums, some of them live and others are studio albums. One is a "best of" and a couple of them are out of print. They can be purchased at their shows, on CDBaby.com or at Bandcamp.com. They are currently working on a new album that is an all Michael Jackson project. They expect it to be released in the summer of 2013.

So, who would enjoy going to a Digdown gig? Erik answered, "I think there is something there for everyone. Young people enjoy the high energy and many of the popular tunes we do. Older people who grew up on big bands really like seeing and hearing the band instruments picked up by the younger generation."

You can find out more about the band at mamadigdown.com or drop an email to mama@mamadigdown.com if you are interested in booking the band for your event.

The coldest and deepest of the five Great Lakes, Lake Superior, is a destination for many fishermen out to catch trout, salmon and walleye. Lake Superior contains over 60 different species of fish.

Both Lake Michigan and Lake Superior have port cities where you can charter a fishing boat for the day with an experienced captain.

Calculate the fish's weight by measuring the girth and length (inches). Use the numbers in this formula: ((girth x girth) x length)/800= lbs.

In April, New London hosts the Big Whopper Weekend fishing contest at Riverside Park. Fish the Wolf River and earn prizes while fishing for walleye, northern and black bass. Food, entertainment and a big raffle are part of the fun-filled weekend.

You certainly don't need a boat to fish. Stand alongside the river or sit on the pier. Some campgrounds have lake or riverside sites where you can fish right from your lawnchair.

You've probably heard about House on the Rock in Spring Green, but have you ever heard of Rock in the House? This attraction, located along Highway 35 in Fountain City, features a 55-ton bolder that rolled down the cliff and plowed right into the house back in 1995.

Instead of removing the rock, the house was turned into a tourist attraction. Park next to the house and walk through and around the outside of the house. No one works here, it's all on the honor system and they ask you to pay one dollar to tour the house. Price is subject to change.

Devil's Lake is a popular destination for rock climbing or rappelling. If you don't care for the equipment and just want to walk around and through rocks, Interstate State Park along the St. Croix River is a great place to do so.

rockclimbing.com is a great source to find other places in Wisconsin to climb and get in touch with others that have experience with these places. devilslakewisconsin.com also has information about climbing at Devil's Lake State Park and local companies that can provide gear, instruction, etc.

Taking a hayride or riding horseback are fun ways to check out the countryside.

Getting above the trees is the best way to take in the beauty of the colorful fall leaves.

Simply watching for wildlife is a popular activity enjoyed by nature enthusiasts in Wisconsin. Groups such as the Madison Audubon Society hold bird watching events and aim to educate and protect their natural habitats.

Wisconsin has thirty different ski destinations surrounded with beautiful scenery, which helps the state earn its rank as third in the US for downhill skiing and snowboarding. Wisconsin also boasts more than 250 trails for cross country skiers.

Natural and man-made hills are converted into sledding fun when there is enough snow to take a fast trip down the hill on your sled.

Fishing is not just for the warm months in Wisconsin. Once the lakes and rivers freeze over, ice fishing is a popular pastime.

The frozen lakes also provide more area to play on snowmobiles and ATVs in the winter.

Saturday Night Preachers

Members of the talented Pratt family, Norm Jr. (Papa Pratt), Jason, Anneliese and Norm III, began their band, Saturday Night Preachers, in 2010. Their first gig was on Saint Patrick's Day that year and they've gone on to perform at festivals, pubs and weddings throughout the Midwest. Their original music cannot be categorized in just one genre – they bring a little folk, alt country, Americana and bluegrass into their tunes.

Brothers, Jason and Norm III, grew up playing music together. They played in a blues band until Jason served four years in the Marine Corps and was stationed in Beaufort, South Carolina. Jason came back to Wisconsin when his time in South Carolina was over and was able to join Norm III in weekly front porch jams once again. It was through these jam sessions that the idea for Saturday Night Preachers formed.

Anneliese, with a truly amazing singing voice, started singing very early in life. She went on to receive a degree in vocal performance at UW-Parkside. With her vocal talent, and being Jason's wife, she was a natural

©Saturday Night Preachers

choice to take lead vocals in the band. Papa Pratt, Jason and Norm's father, played music in his living room for 37 years until his sons dragged him on stage during a gig in 2009. Papa Pratt joined the band and plays guitar and harmonica. Jason plays the upright bass and Norm plays guitar, banjo and mandolin. Everyone in the band contributes to the vocals. They admit that being a family band has its challenges, but they have also used it as an opportunity to understand one another better.

Norm III explains their musical influences, "Punch Brothers certainly raised our eyebrows on having bluegrass instrumentation (banjo/mandolin/ guitar/ bass fiddle) and creating outside the bluegrass standard ideas. Steve Earle (pictured with Norm on the left) has left his musical mark in our style too. We're pretty eclectic as far as what we listen to and I think we're influenced by just about everything we hear."

Saturday Night Preachers just released their first CD, "If We Leave Here Tonight," which is available through their website (saturdaynightpreachers. com) and a few local record shops in Milwaukee. They hope to build up their original music repertoire and we can hopefully expect a lot more from them in the future.

©Saturday Night Preachers

The band regularly plays at the YardArm Pub and Grill and McAuliff's on the Square in Racine. They've also started playing at festivals in the Milwaukee area such as Bastille Days, Sizzling' Saturdays in the Third Ward, Party on the Pavement in Racine and the East Troy Bluegrass Festival.

If you'd like to contact the Saturday Night Preachers for an event, you can contact them through their website, saturdaynightpreachers.com or email them at saturdaynightpreachers@hotmail.com.

©Saturday Night Preachers

©Kelly Maddern

wildlife . nature

Wisconsin is full of critters of all sizes, types and colors. They are not only interesting to learn about, but they are also fun to see out in their natural habitat. Once you learn about their habits and start paying attention, you'll be surprised at all of the animal activity going on around you. The animals are often well hidden in their surroundings, but as you start teaching your eye what to look for, finding the animals will become easier and easier.

Here in Wisconsin, we are lucky to have so many people who are dedicated to preserving our wildlife and their natural surroundings. Many groups help injured animals recover or live out their life with their injuries in the best way possible. These groups also educate others and provide continual support and training for volunteers who take on these important roles. Other groups get together to enjoy wildlife watching or photography together and learn from one another.

There is a lot more to Wisconsin's wildlife than you will find at the bar on a Saturday night. Ba-dum ching.

Geese often go back to the same general location each year at nesting time. The male and the female mate for life, unless something happens to one of them, in which case they will usually find a new mate. This couple came back to their same nesting area in the middle of a busy parking lot.

The female tends to the nest and the male stays nearby, always on alert, to protect the female and the nest.

After the female lays her 4-7 eggs, she doesn't leave the nest other than to get a quick bite to eat or to bathe.

Once the goslings are born, the father becomes more laid back and social with the other geese.

The goslings are led to water within a day of being born. Here they will learn to swim and use the water to protect themselves from predators.

Geese go through an 8-10 week flightless period during the summer when they molt. Molting is when they lose their wing feathers and regrow new ones. During this time they stay near the water for protection from predators since they are unable to fly.

By standing on one foot, geese (and other birds) keep warm. They lose body heat through their legs, so they tuck one in close to prevent heat loss.

Geese fly in a "V" formation to conserve energy, to keep an eye on all the birds in the flock and for best communication between the birds.

Hundreds of geese stand on the thin ice, near the open water. These geese are considered resident geese and do not leave in the winter with the migratory flocks.

If you enter the marsh at the auto tour area, off of highway 49 east of Waupun, you can stop and take a walk through some of the marsh on the floating boardwalk. While on your walk, be sure to look around - you should see all sorts of different animals that call the marsh home.

The boardwalk is sturdy and large enough to fit a wheelchair.

As one of the largest freshwater marshes in the US, the Horicon Marsh measures 3,000 acres. It is also a popular migration stop for geese.

This gazebo is a nice place to stop along the floating boardwalk and use the provided scopes to look for birds or other animals.

The Feather Rehabilitation Center

The Feather Rehabilitation Center in New London was started in 1987 by Patricia Fisher. The center is a place where sick, injured or orphaned wild birds can be placed to receive care and hopefully be rehabilitated and released back into the wild. The Feather also provides education to school kids and the general public about wildlife and the birds.

In 1988, Don Baumgartner came to Pat looking for some advice about bluebirds. After he asked what was in the large cage in Pat's front yard and seeing the red-tailed hawk named Anny, Don was hooked. Don has been a very important volunteer for The Feather, as there is not a thing he hasn't done to help the birds. Since then, a handful of other volunteers have joined the crew and each one lends a big hand to keep the center up and running.

In 1991, The Feather applied for federal and state permits and received their 501c3 status. The cages were all built with grant money, back when the economy was doing better. They now rely primarily on donations in order to feed the birds, update the cages, and for other needs as they arise.

Pat spends two hours and fifteen minutes each day doing chores for all of the birds. She says that she rarely leaves New London because of this great responsibility, but if she does, there are people she can rely on to take care of the birds in her absence.

Pat spoke specifically about a crane with myopathy that they rehabbed and released. The crane's name was Ms. Earl and when she was released, she went back to be with her mate, who was waiting for her. "Makes it all seem worth it," Pat said about that story, "It's a love-hate relationship. We love them; they hate us."

All of the cages have handicap access for the birds who can't fly. They have a variety of perches at various levels which allow them to hop up to where they want to go. One of the cages is 120 feet, divided into three 40 foot sections. Another pen is 24 feet and can be divided into three sections. The 60 foot pen is for the educational birds at The Feather. The 28 foot pen is permanently divided into two sections and a 40 foot pen can be divided into three pens.

Over half of the rehab center is dedicated to Sandhill Cranes. There are five indoor heated pens for the sandhills, for those who need to stay over the winter. There is an outdoor area with a top net where the cranes can go before they are capable of flying. The birds are always put away at night to keep them safe from predators.

For more information about The Feather Rehabilitation Center, visit their website at www.thefeather.org. Consider making a donation while you are on the website so they can continue to do what they do for these birds. You can also watch Ms. Harvey on a webcam at livewildlifecams.com by clicking on Ms Harvey in the top left corner.

Sharkey, Red-Tailed Hawk, caught in power lines.

Baum, Great Horned Owl, has a bad eye, is a surrogate mother for owl eggs.

Azio Blaze, Short Earred Owl, was hit by a car and has a bad eye and bad wing.

Ebony Rose, Turkey Vulture, was imprinted as a human, doesn't know she's a vulture.

Autumn, Great Horned Owl, missing a wing tip.

Savannah, Barred Owl, has been a successful surrogate to some young owls.

Pirate, Bald Eagle, was born in 1978.

Ms. Harvey, Great Horned Owl, raised illegally by humans, has her own babies and takes care of surrogates.

Bella, Saw Whet Owl, with Pat Fisher.

Ghost, Snowy Owl, bad eye and missing wing.

Seneca, Red-Tailed Hawk, was shot and had a hurt left foot, which was fixed, and right wing that wasn't fixed.

GrayWind, Sandhill Crane, blind in one eye and a surrogate mother to colts each spring.

Turkey vultures live all over Wisconsin. They usually do not kill their food, they eat roadkill or animals that have died from disease.

Turkey vultures don't have a voice box, so they have no call. They do make grunting or hissing sounds.

These birds, which date back to prehistoric times, were thought to be in the bird of prey family. DNA proves they are in the stork family.

Like an owl, vultures regurgitate pellets of the indigestible parts of their food. They also vomit when they are upset.

The Bald Eagle was once on Wisconsin's endangered species list, but was removed from the list in 1997. These majestic birds can be found around lakes and rivers in the northern two-thirds of the state.

Pairs of eagles mate for life and both parents will incubate the eggs. Their nest can reach up to 6 feet wide after years of building up the same nest. The males are generally smaller than the females.

Osprey, otherwise known as the fish hawk, spend their summers in northern and north central Wisconsin.

While incubating the eggs, the female Osprey will rarely leave the nest. The male will bring food to her.

Osprey hover over water to watch for fish. They dive, feet first, and snag the fish in their sharp claws. Because of this fish diet, you will mostly see the birds along waterways. Their nests, typically about 3 feet wide, are easy to recognize at the top of tall trees.

Red-Tailed Hawks are a common sight in the lower 2/3 of Wisconsin. They are often seen on power poles or trees on the edge of a field.

A hawk's eyesight is eight times greater than a human's, which is helpful for catching mice 100 feet away.

This free-range Guinea Fowl is raised on a farm and serves as an alarm when predators are near. They can also be eaten.

With exception to far northern Wisconsin, wild turkeys can be found roaming in wooded areas around the state.

Mallard ducks are one of the most recognizable and abundant breeds throughout the world. Males are colorful and females are brown.

Female Wood Duck with her babies. With the help of people creating Wood Duck boxes, the once declining population is increasing again.

These ducks and geese sit along the beach in Port Washington.

This Whooping Crane, an endangered species, can be seen at the International Crane Foundation in Baraboo.

The International Crane Foundation is home to the only collection of all 15 species of cranes in the world.

Cranes have a very loud and distinct call. They have alarm calls, a flight intention call and a unison call in their vocabulary.

Sandhill Cranes have a wingspan of 6 or 7 feet and the Whooping Crane, the larger of the two breeds, has a wingspan of 7.5 feet.

Scott Weberpal Nature & Wildlife Photography

Scott Weberpal has been interested in photography as far back as he can remember. He grew up on a pig farm near Janesville, on the Rock Prairie, where the skies are endless. It was upon this landscape he began photographing the skyscapes and weather phenomena around him.

Scott's main interests lie in photographing wildlife and severe weather, but the time, patience and equipment required haven't been available to him until recent years. Regarding these favorite subjects, Scott claims, "Both present a significant challenge, but capturing that ultimate shot of either, in my opinion, is an amazing reward as a photographer."

Scott's favorite spot in Wisconsin to take photos is the Horicon Marsh. The variety of wildlife and the ease of access to some areas of the marsh can't be found anywhere else in the state. Otherwise, he suggests the Kettle Moraine State Forest as being fantastic with varying wildlife, terrain and vegetation types. During the spring and summer, Scott spends a lot of time chasing severe weather across the country… largely in the Great Plains.

Scott has a 13-year-old son and works as a Geographic Information Systems Technician. With the amount of time and patience needed for his photography, it really limits how much time he can spend out in nature. For now, he is going to keep photography as a hobby, but, in the near future, he hopes to have a more extensive portfolio so he can set up a website where prints can be ordered. Currently, his images can be viewed on Facebook at: facebook.com/ScottWeberpalPhotography.

For other aspiring photographers, Scott suggests, "Be patient, be very patient. Don't try to be like anyone else, find your own niche and roll with it."

Each image Scott Weberpal provided for this book, over the next few pages, has been photographed within Wisconsin's borders.

© Scott Weberpal Photography

© Scott Weberpal Photography

© Scott Weberpal Photography

© Scott Weberpal Photography

The Baltimore Oriole can be attracted to your yard with oranges cut in half. The Red Breasted Grosbeak is an insect eater.

The beautiful yellow finch, along with other types of finches, can be attracted to your yard with sunflowers and thistle seed.

10 species of woodpeckers can be found throughout the state. The holes in this tree are where a Pileated Woodpecker most-likely pecked.

Baby Mourning Doves, like the one above, leave the nest two weeks after hatching. These male cardinals are fighting near a coveted birdfeeder.

The American Robin is Wisconsin's state bird. The robin is one of the earliest bird species to lay eggs after migrating from their winter region. Wisconsinites often gauge when spring has arrived after the long, cold winter by the sighting of a Robin.

The Robin will have two to three broods during the nesting season, which ranges from April to July.

The Robin's eggs are a distinct blue color and each clutch typically consists of 3-5 eggs.

Discovery Center in Manitowish Waters

The non-profit Discovery Center, which formed in 1996, is a Northwoods, nature-based education and community center located in Manitowish Waters. The beautiful grounds consist of a lake, river, mixed forest and a bog. The center is a place for adults, children and families to enjoy and learn about the surrounding environment.

©Katie Simonsen

This unique center is available to the public as well as groups, schools and events. The member-based organization receives over half of their operational dollars through donor, foundation and member support. The center also applies for grants to help support programming and hosts at least two fundraisers each year. The rest of the money is earned income from programs, facility rentals and retail sales. It is because of these incoming funds that they can offer complimentary use of their fishing poles, kayaks, canoes, rowboats, sail boats, beautiful beach and swimming area. Basketball, sand volleyball, trail hiking and a nature center with live animals are also available at no cost.

Instructor-led activities and nature programs are offered year round, some free and some with a minimal fee. Some of these events include: bird banding, butterfly tagging, bat monitoring, guided ecology hikes and snowshoes, eco-cultural pontoon rides and canoe trips, adult lecture series, youth eco-learning camps and day programs, trail celebration days, lake health training, birding festival, wilderness triathlon, photography workshops, yoga and zumba.

©Katie Simonsen

The Discovery Center also hosts community-minded events like socials, dinner-and-a-speaker, family fun days, as well as lake association picnics and meetings, family reunions, camp groups, and weddings. Their trails are open to hiking and biking in the summer and are groomed for cross-country skiing in the winter.

A staff of seven year-round (five full-time) and some seasonal staff (primarily interns) keep the year-round center in operation. During the summer of 2012, they had five additional paid summer staff. The center also has an active board of directors and a volunteer corps that help to teach programs, work the front desk, organize their annual events and fundraisers, send out mailings, tend to gardens and more.

Though there are quite a few nature centers throughout the state, the Discovery Center strives to set themselves apart by the extra care they give to their site, encouraging drop-in use and wanting the entire site to be utilized and viewed as an asset to the region and beyond. Their mission is "to enrich lives and inspire an ethic of care for Wisconsin's Northwoods, through the facilitation of connections among people, nature, and community." This mission is a bit more encompassing than many nature centers, as they don't solely lead nature programs. The center provides an atmosphere where visitors and the community are influenced by the their positive nature ethic.

©Kelly Maddern

Because much of the summer activities in the Northwoods are focused in and around the lakes – especially on nice, warm and sunny days – those can often be the best days to visit the Discovery Center. The drop-in traffic is never very busy, so there is a chance you and your friends or family could feel like you have the place to yourselves. The Discovery Center's busiest week of the year is usually early July, around Independence Day. Their annual triathlon is always the Saturday before the 4th and then they host their Family Fun Day following the 4th of

©Katie Simonsen

July. Additionally, Wine in the Woods, their annual fundraiser, is always hosted in mid-July. The Wine in the Woods event features music on the amphitheater, wine, an outdoor dinner and a live and silent auction. Members donate bottles of wine (with values up to $3000) to auction off. The proceeds support their programming and general operations costs throughout the year.

The center is currently working on getting some live education animals, including bats and birds of prey. They recently received their permits to house education bats and are working on that as one of their upcoming projects.

To learn more about the Discovery Center, please visit www.discoverycenter.net.

Whitetail Deer can run up to 40 mph and swim up to 13 mph. Their tail, when straight up, tells the others to run for safety.

This Whitetail Deer, only 5 ft. from us, was unalarmed and continued on with its business as we walked by.

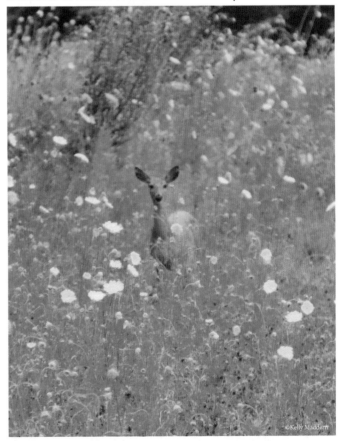

Deer prefer to live in forests or near fields of crops to have easy access to safety and food. Deer hunting is a popular sport in Wisconsin.

Does give birth to fawns in May or June each year. The doe will have one to three fawns per year.

Wisconsin is home to 11 species of turtles. Once their eggs have hatched, you may see a scattering of eggs around the nest like above.

The Painted Turtle, top, is the most common turtle in Wisconsin. Wisconsin has 12 frog and 1 toad species. This is the gray tree frog.

Wisconsin snakes stay through the winter and hibernate. Since they rely on the environment for heat, you may see them basking in the sun.

18 species of snakes call Wisconsin home. Most are harmless and very colorful. Two species of rattlesnake are venomous but rare.

If you really love butterflies, go to a butterfly garden such as the one at Olbrich Gardens in Madison or at the Milwaukee Public Museum.

These big, noisy creatures are cicadas. You hear their loud hum in the summer, usually an indication that autumn is on its way.

This is the Black Swallowtail butterfly, which is a common species in Wisconsin. It likes to eat dill, parsley, parsnip and carrots.

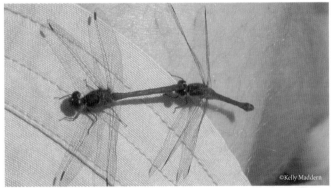

Approximately 110 species of dragonflies can be found in Wisconsin. The Hine's Emerald Dragonfly is on Wisconsin's endangered list.

More than 500 species of spiders can be found in Wisconsin. The largest they get is about 1.5 inches for the body length.

Japanese beetles are a destructive pest to many types of plants by eating their flowers and leaves.

Wisconsin has 10 different types of squirrels, including this one, the gray squirrel. There are two species of flying squirrels in the state.

The Red Fox is very common throughout Wisconsin. They eat 1-2 pounds of food per day, which includes rodents and small animals.

Occasionally, you come across an albino squirrel like this one in Delafield.

This giant paper wasp nest was built from the branch of a tree.

Here, paper wasps busily work around their hive. This is at the beginning of summer, not long after the queen built the new nest.

In 1977, the honeybee was identified as the state insect. Wisconsin ranks 9th in the nation for honey production.

Ralph Curtis Photography

I am continually reminded how small of a world it is, especially here in Wisconsin. A friend of mine suggested that I check out Ralph Curtis' photography. Not a week later, a coworker suggested I check out Ralph's photography as well, and those two people don't know each other. I certainly couldn't ignore the recommendations. When I first saw his photos, I was not only mesmerized, I was hooked. I couldn't wait to see what he would produce next. With my love of photography, I wanted to know how he does what he does and how I could capture images that are anything near the quality of his. Since Ralph lives not far from me I wanted to know how I could also experience this type of natural beauty first-hand, practically in my own backyard.

© Ralph Curtis Photography

Ralph Curtis has had an interest in photography his whole life, but it wasn't until 2007 that he had become passionate about this hobby. His love of bird-watching and deer hunting helped him to learn how to get closer to wildlife with the camera. As a Photoshop technician by trade, retouching images for companies such as National Geographic, Vanity Fair, Victoria Secret, LL Bean and Kohl's grew his interest in photography significantly. In 2009, he finally took the plunge on some professional equipment, and his passion continued to grow. Ralph, not wanting to make his photography seem like work, said he has no plans for it to become a full-time gig. He does plan to sell more images when he retires so it can be supplemental income.

When not working or spending time out in nature, Ralph volunteers for Waukesha County Land Conservancy and is the coordinator for their deer management program. Whitetail deer are one of his favorite subjects to photograph, and, more specifically, he loves to capture images of mature bucks because they are hard to get close to in the wild. As one who enjoys a challenge, Ralph will only photograph in the wild and not at places such as deer farms. Additionally, he enjoys photographing songbirds, herons and egrets.

With a love for Wisconsin and its diversity, Ralph is happy to do photography anywhere in the state. Most of his photography is done close to home, in the southeast area of Wisconsin, since time and preparation are easier. The Horicon Marsh, in central Wisconsin, or the Crex Meadows, in northwest Wisconsin, are a couple of places he suggests as the best places to get nature photos within the state.

Because I, personally, love his work so much, I had to ask him how he did it and what equipment he uses. Ralph uses Canon cameras, mainly because it was his first camera and he thinks their lenses are superior. He suggests, "Learn as much as you can about your subject, their habits, their senses, their daily rituals. It is so important to be in position for a shot before the wildlife even shows up. You capture wildlife acting naturally, instead of being too far away for a fleeting glimpse."

Over time, Ralph's photography has turned some corners in regards to quality. The more he does it, the better each image becomes. He aspires to become more artistic with his imagery and to move beyond being just a wildlife portrait photographer.

Ralph does have images for sale on his website, www.ralphcurtis.com, where gallery wraps or prints can be ordered. The very latest of his photos can be viewed on his Facebook page. (facebook.com/ralph.curtis.photography) You may even run into his images while reading a magazine or periodical somewhere in the Midwest.

Each image Ralph Curtis provided for this book, over the next few pages, has been photographed within Wisconsin's borders.

© Ralph Curtis Photography

© Ralph Curtis Photography

© Ralph Curtis Photography

© Ralph Curtis Photography

© Ralph Curtis Photography

© Ralph Curtis Photography

©Kelly Maddern

weather . seasons

There is a saying in Wisconsin, "If you don't like the weather, wait five minutes." It may seem like an exaggeration, but there are times when the adage isn't far off the mark.

Wisconsin weather is: sun, clouds, blizzards, tornadoes, sub-zero temperatures, blistering heat, ice storms, severe thunderstorms, high winds, no winds, droughts, floods, rainbows, hail, thundersnow, and almost everything else in between. The summers are short, the winters are long, and, for some, it is the exact opposite. In the spring, it's time to head outside for the first time in many months. Come fall, it is comforting to bundle up for trips to the apple orchard, to see the fall colors and to find the best Halloween pumpkins.

If you didn't know, Wisconsin only has two seasons... Winter and road construction. Now you know.

WiNTeR

On the cold side of Wisconsin's extreme spectrum, winter can get as cold as -30°F. Typically, the average high temperature is around 20°F in the middle of the season. With the northern edge of Wisconsin along Lake Superior, lake-effect snows create a large amount of snow that is not typical across the rest of the state. On average, northern Wisconsin may see over 100 inches of snow versus only 30 inches in the south. The winter playground is great for skiing, snowboarding, snowmobiling, ice fishing, sledding, ice boating and using your garage as an extra freezer.

©Kelly Maddern

©Kelly Maddern

©Kelly Maddern

©Kelly Maddern

©Kelly Maddern

©Kelly Maddern

SPRING

The awakening of spring is an exciting time in Wisconsin. After the long, cold winter, everyone is ready to get outside, open up their houses and spend time in their gardens once again. The first warm days of the year are the long-awaited end of a several-month hibernation. The parks are full of kids, bikers and runners fill the trails, and establishments bring out their outdoor seating. Trees begin to bud, flowers begin to bloom – the state is alive again.

SUMMER

Summer, on the other side of Wisconsin's extreme weather spectrum, is the hottest time of the year. With temperatures that can exceed 100°, but often stay in the 80s and 90s, summer is the time of year where lake activities, camping, Northwoods vacations and any other methods of enjoying the outdoors are popular in Wisconsin. The blazing sun, paired with the high humidity, can be the perfect recipe for some exciting summer storms.

MidWest Severe Storm Tracking/Response Center

During a warm summer evening just after my high school graduation in 1996, I encountered something so powerful and scary that it paved the way for my future desire to help my community. As I played co-ed softball at a rural baseball diamond in Ladoga, an unexpected line of rain and thunder formed right over us – in an otherwise blue sky. As the line grew thicker north of us and began to move southeast, the clouds rumbled continuously and began to swirl. Between downpours, we attempted to finish our game. Over the loud rumble of thunder, the left fieldman attempted to get our attention by yelling and waving wildly. We ran to where he stood, just beyond the visual obstruction of the house and trees to the east of the ball diamond. In front of us, not more than a quarter to a half-mile away, was a huge, well-formed tornado. What I witnessed that day was an F5 tornado that ravaged Oakfield and left a vivid memory, forever etched in my head.

It was years later, after college when I moved to Madison, that I decided to further pursue my interest in severe weather. I contacted Madison Area Science and Technology (MAST) and set up some one-on-one time with the head of the organization to take their Advanced Spotter Training class. After receiving my certification through MAST, I connected with the owner of MidWestSSTRC (MidWest Severe Storm Tracking/Response Center), an organization that was still in its infancy. I was offered a position on the Board of Directors and worked hard with the other board members to create a group that would benefit the citizens of Dane County.

Unfortunately, after some time with the group, I had to move away from Madison. But, still today, Dale (Berny) Bernstein runs the group he began, and they continue to become stronger and more involved.

Left to Right: Chad Woodward, Steve Fitzsimmons and Dale Bernstein on the radio.
©MidWestSSTRC

Berny wrote this about MidWestSSTRC:

"From days of long ago to the present and beyond to the future,there has been and will be a need for the volunteer. The volunteer is only as effective as the support surrounding that person or group of persons.

"As the President/CEO of the MidWestSSTRC, my personal interest of severe storm involvement traces back to 1967 and continued to 1983 when I committed my company of National Fire & Safety, Ltd. to volunteer people and resources for the purpose of early severe storm warnings. The relaying of accurate and up-to-the-minute info is an integral and essential ingredient to this focus. This is now what is referred to as providing ground truth. MidWestSSTRC, Inc. is a noncommercial, non-profit organization of volunteers, whose goal is to help to develop the best possible severe weather warning system possible. We have come a long way from having to stop and use pay phones, to using the first cellular phones, to now having use of our own FM Business Band radio frequency and sharing the air waves with the Amateur Radio/HAM, with the advantage of these communications networks the MidWest AOR continues to grow.

"Those reports include, yet are not limited to: the occurrence of tornadoes, funnel clouds, large hail, damaging straight-line winds, flash floods, etc. The reporting is done both in real-time and after-the-fact, in providing what is referred to as 'ground truth' for severe weather events and weather phenomena. Post-event evaluations are also an important function of MidWestSSTRC.

"From 1983 to the present, while working with committed severe storm groups and individuals, we have seen a need and direction to become even more committed, to become professional in our efforts and involvement that focuses on Severe Storm Tracking and Response.

"The concept of the MidWest Severe Storm Tracking/Response Center was born out of this direction. Over two years of discussions and planning had laid the groundwork for this non-profit organization. In essence, MidWestSSTRC has been in existence since 1983.

"Our purpose and existence is to-the-point. A professional and knowing means of assisting in the early warning of severe storms, the proper response and the professional, accurate means of relaying storm information; that those efforts assist in protecting life and property.

"Our future goals are many and include the response to severe storms and how we as an organization will be able to lend assistance to those who request. We are pleased to announce that MidWestSSTRC is a member of the National Association for Search and Rescue as a first step of meeting these goals that we have set. Additionally, we have added the MidWest Disaster Assessment Team (D.A.T), of which we assist the National Weather Service and other recognized entities in performing post event Damage Assessments. MidWest has also been conferring with the WI Civil Air Patrol for aerial surveys with training flights.

"MidWestSSTRC continues to offer assistance to local severe storm spotter groups, the National Weather Service and other organizations with field information as we commit numerous personnel and resources to this effort at any given time, in and around Wisconsin. Individual lifestyle schedules continue to be problematic in training schedules with local spotter groups and also for obtaining additional needed volunteers and we welcome all those who have an interest in joining MidWest on any level.

"MidWestSSTRC has committed personnel to attend various conferences and training over the years and will continue to do so as they become available.

"What we do is not a sport; nor is it to be taken lightly. Although there are lighter moments in what we do, the situation can and does become a serious matter to be dealt with professionally and expeditiously. Often times very little happens. But when things start to happen, one must be trained and prepared to serve the community in the best means possible. So if this is something that interests you, come on board, we'd love to have ya. Remember, be safe, be knowledgeable, and be prepared.

"Our Mission Statement:
The MidWest Severe Storm Tracking Response Center (MidWestSSTRC Inc.) is comprised of members whose primary purpose is to assist in providing early detection of severe weather. We communicate this critical information to government officials, other recognized agencies and organizations including the National Weather Service allowing for timely public severe weather warnings and providing emergency responses as appropriate. MidWest SSTRC Inc. endeavors to assist in any way it can in the protection of life and property from any threat, be it natural or manmade.

MidWest SSTRC Inc. – A 501c3 Non-profit Corporation"

For more information about where to find MidWestSSTRC or how to become involved, visit their website at www.midwestsstrc.org.

eagle TORNαDO, 2010

On June 21, 2010, amid a severe weather outbreak, an F2 tornado hit the town of Eagle with winds as strong as 125-130 miles per hour. The storm barreled through at 9:15pm and caused damage to 125 homes, 25 of those completely leveled, but fortunately no fatalities. This event, like other natural disasters that have happened in Wisconsin, demonstrated the strong sense of community and willingness to lend a hand to a neighbor in need.

©Kelly Maddern

©Kelly Maddern

©Kelly Maddern

©Kelly Maddern

©Kelly Maddern

*au*TU*MN*

Like spring, the fall is a time of transition, from the hot summer to the cold winter. After months of heat, the cool weather is welcome and the harvest traditions begin. Apple orchards, pumpkins, hayrides, turning of the fall leaves and enjoying the outdoors as much as possible are typical autumn activities. Before you know it, Halloween and Thanksgiving have passed by and the ground is covered in snow.

©Kelly Maddern

SMALL BUSINESS

Wisconsin is made up of hundreds of thousands of small businesses of all shapes, sizes and types. In fact, many Wisconsinites and visitors alike tour towns throughout the state because of the selection of local shops, restaurants and recreational attractions.

With this book, my main goal was to share photos and information about places to go off the beaten path, while also placing a focus on small businesses. We have very passionate, ambitious and creative people in Wisconsin and it is evident through their endeavors.

I encourage you to shop locally and support Wisconsin farmers and small business owners. There are a few easy ways to find local companies or Wisconsin-made products: refer to the Something Special from Wisconsin website mentioned at the beginning of this book, do an internet search for Wisconsin companies and products, or plan to shop at the local farmers' market each week.

If you are way up north, along Lake Superior, look for Boudreau's Antiques and Collectibles east of Ashland along Hwy 2. Don't bother looking for a name on the place; I promise you'll recognize it just by looking at this picture.

Many of you will know exactly what this place is within two seconds of seeing the photo. For those of you who don't know, it is one of those places that should be on a must-see list for Wisconsin. This is Al Johnson's Swedish restaurant in Sister Bay, Door County. (And, yes, they are real!)

Here is a tiny piece of the Jack's Cafe grounds in Waukesha. It's a hidden gem with fantastic food and shopping.

At harvest time, between late August and October, you can visit local farms to pick apples and pumpkins. The farms range from very small to large like below.

An example of a fairly large harvest-time attraction is the Elegant Farmer in Mukwonago. Activities include: hayrides, apple picking, pumpkin picking, pony rides, making caramel apples, shopping and a food tent. It is a popular place in the fall.

Pieper Porch Winery & Vineyard

Pieper Porch Winery and Vineyard is a very new winery, just opened in May of 2012. Located in Mukwonago, one and a half miles east of highway 83, the winery is just off of scenic River Road and overlooks the Vernon Marsh. The winery is family-owned and operated, and the tasting room is built on to the back of Todd and Kathy Pieper's residence.

Because they are so new, they are in the process of building and growing their vineyard. They will grow Marquette grapes, a red variety that was developed at the University of Minnesota to handle the cold temperatures of the northern states. In the meantime, and in addition to their future grapes, the Pieper's use purchased grapes, Door County cherries and Warrens cranberries along with other purchased fruits and juices to make over ten varieties of wines.

They make red wines such as their **River Road Red**, which is a Cabernet/Merlot, lightly oaked and great paired with a roast or barbequed steak. The **Red Fox** is a Zinfandel/Shiraz blend that finishes with a peppery spice and goes well with spicy foods.

Their white wines vary from a dry Pinot Gris called the **Willow Run**, which is great with a light dinner or pasta, to the **Marshland**, which is a Moscato, a sweet dessert wine. The **Marsh Moon** is a clean, crisp and cool Riesling and the **Winding Road White** is a Sauvignon Blanc, which is medium-bodied, crisp, refreshing and excellent with seafood.

©Kelly Maddern

©Kelly Maddern

Their **"Porch Wines"** are a variety of fruit wines, including some 2012 Wisconsin State Fair award winners:

• The **Pieper Porch Apple Wine** is winemaker Todd's very own recipe, an all American wine.

• The **Pieper Porch Black Currant** is a bronze medal winner. This bold, rich wine uses black currants brought in from the Pacific Northwest and is excellent with dark chocolate and almonds.

• The **Pieper Porch Black Raspberry** is an easy-drinking wine and tastes and smells just like fresh-picked raspberries.

• The **Pieper Porch Blueberry** wine is a combination of blueberries, apple juice and Pinot Noir, which creates a sweet and intense fruit flavor. The Door County cherries are combined with Pinot Noir juice to create a semi-sweet Pieper Porch Cherry wine that is great with ham.

• Warrens cranberries, mixed with apples, are used to make the **Pieper Porch Cranberry**, a bronze medal winner. This sweet-tart wine goes well with turkey, pork and grilled foods.

• The **Pieper Porch Lemon**, a silver medal winner, is a very popular wine. It is described as "a summer day in a wine glass." It's a refreshing wine that should be served chilled.

• The **Pieper Porch Strawberry** wine is full of flavor and aroma and has a crisp finish.

• For a nice combination of fruit flavors, the **Pieper Porch Vernon Sunset** is a sweet Sangria with notes of orange, lemon, lime and cherry.

• The **Pieper Porch Winter Apple** wine is full of apples and spice and is great served warm, especially on a cold Wisconsin night.

When you visit the Porch, you can take a tour of their winemaking area and spend some time in the tasting room, sampling some of their many varieties of wine. There are tables set up in the tasting room for you to relax and enjoy the samples, or purchase a glass or a bottle to enjoy while you sit. The Porch is an inviting area to sit outside, with a beautiful view of the marsh. The Piepers invite you to bring a snack or pack a lunch to enjoy on the porch or inside while you sip your wine.

If you want more information about the winery, help to find the location or to get in touch with Todd or Kathy Pieper, visit their website at www.pieperporchwines.com.

Dave's BrewFarm

"Farmer" Dave Anderson dreamed up the BrewFarm concept back in 1995. In 2008, after spending many months looking for the perfect location, Dave finally broke ground in Wilson, Wisconsin, and began to establish his sustainably-based craft brewery.

On February 3, 2009, a Jacobs 31-20, 20 kW wind generator, was raised on the farm. "Jake" stands 120 feet tall and is expected to provide up to 50% of the electricity that is used between the brewery and the house. Dave also uses geothermal heating and cooling and solar panels for thermal water heating. He recycles the brewery wastewater, which is then used in the hopyard and the Little Wold Farmstead's orchards. Little Wolf Farmstead is the agricultural side of the business, where Dave grows hops, fruit, spices, herbs and vegetables. The produce grown here can be used to create beers with unique flavors.

©Dave's BrewFarm

Dave hopes he can lead by example and provide a renewable and sustainable business practice that encourages other businesses to do the same. Dave is the only one that works at the BrewFarm, and he plans to keep it that way. His business was conceived and designed to be a one-person operation that is more lifestyle-oriented than growth-oriented.

©Dave's BrewFarm

The BrewFarm is a laid-back atmosphere that attracts beer lovers. It's small and intimate; Dave likens it to a church basement, but with tasty beer. People bring food, their grills and they hang out. It's a great place to meet new friends and have a great time.

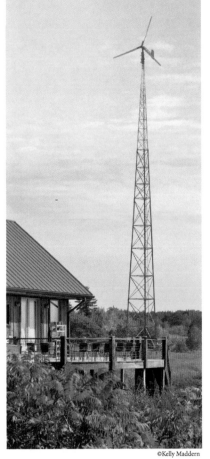

©Kelly Maddern

When Dave was asked what, exactly, he brews at the BrewFarm, he responded, "It's more like 'what don't I brew'. My beers are quite non-traditional and don't fit into a style that's easily labeled. Amorphous."

BrewFarm beers are currently only available at the brewery, but Dave expects that to change soon. Occasionally, you can find the BrewFarm at festivals, like the Great Taste of the Midwest, which Dave says is the best festival in the country.

If you are looking to head out to the BrewFarm, the hours vary and you can find the hours posted on Dave's BrewFarm Facebook page or on the blog at www.brewfarm.com. The farm is located at 2470 Wilson Street, Wilson, WI 54027, or you can use the GPS coordinates: +44° 58' 24.90", -92° 10' 33.06"

BOBROWITZ SCULPTURES

On a random road trip in February, the kids and I passed a sign that said "Spectacular Sculpture." A half-mile past the sign, I had the urge to turn around and follow the sign to see what we'd find.

©Kelly Maddern

The first sign pointed me down a road to the next sign, which led me into a residential neighborhood. I looked for other cars, or a gathering of people, to indicate where this spectacular sculpture might be. In all, we came across three different signs, and after the third, we had reached a dead end. Ahead of us wound a long driveway full of metal sculptures. The kids' eyes got big, as did mine, and we slowly drove down the long driveway until we reached a house and a turnaround in the driveway. The signs along the drive told us to park and look around, so we did.

As we walked around the side of the house and to the backyard, we saw a sea of sculptures in the yard, on the sides of several outbuildings, in the trees and on the roofs of the buildings. There had to have been hundreds, if not thousands, of sculptures of all sizes, colors and materials. We spent nearly an hour looking around before we left, and I knew I was going to have to contact the person or people who owned all of these brilliant pieces of art. Though the signs said that they were open from sunrise to sunset, we were there on a whim and I did not want to disturb them on a Saturday afternoon. Upon returning home, I immediately contacted Paul and we arranged a time to meet.

PAUL BOBROWITZ, SCULPTOR

©Kelly Maddern

Mr. Paul Bobrowitz realized through his personal awareness therapy that he needed more fun and creativity in his life. The rigidity of his upbringing no longer suited him, and he chose to leave his career as a carpenter to make sculptures his full-time passion.

When Paul first started creating sculptures over twenty years ago as a hobby, he used old farm equipment and took down old barns to repurpose the materials. He later added industrial scrap to his arsenal of materials, and now uses nearly anything that he can get his hands on and envision a new life for.

Paul and his wife, Sandy, built the home they currently live in. Paul had only planned to stay in this house for about ten years, but now, close to thirty years later, they remain in what has also become a large art gallery featuring the hundreds of sculptures he had created over the years. Paul estimates that about 3 acres of the over 6 acres of land they own is dedicated to displaying the sculptures. Paul and his wife have recently had conversations of moving from this home. Though a very daunting task to move all of the sculptures, Paul doesn't appear concerned – they will get through it "one sculpture at a time."

©Kelly Maddern

When the Bobrowitzes first bought the land they live on, it was an open hay field. Paul planted trees and created a yard that is now beautifully wooded and home to birds, squirrels, fox and other wildlife. The look and feel of each sculpture benefits from these natural surroundings. Rusty sculptures look beautiful against the white snow of winter and stainless steel sculptures glisten beautifully in the sun against the fall colors of the trees. All of the Wisconsin elements – frost, rain, sun, snow – enhance the beauty of each sculpture. Paul has also witnessed how the look and feel of a sculpture can change dramatically when transplanted from his gallery to someone's yard.

The sculpture gallery has attracted visitors of all sorts. Car clubs, motorcycle clubs, nursing homes, bus tours, schools, photographers, musicians and scavenger hunts are just a small example of groups that have come to view and appreciate the art Paul has created. The Bobrowitz sculptures are also available for lease and have been on display at churches, festivals and in municipalities. Paul has gone to schools, after they visited his gallery, to work with the students and build sculptures of their own. The students bring in materials that they choose, and Paul shows them how they can recycle their garbage into works of art.

©Kelly Maddern

The sculpture gallery, located in Colgate, Wisconsin, is a prime example of the treasures you can find off the beaten path throughout the state. It is a display that must be experienced first-hand to appreciate the hard work, craftsmanship and creativity that has gone in to these sculptures. The vast collection of hundreds of sculptures will certainly amaze you, as you could spend hours looking through the pieces and still feel like you haven't seen everything Paul Bobrowitz has to share. To find out more about Paul and his sculpture gallery, visit his website www.bobrowitzsculpture.com.

©Kelly Maddern

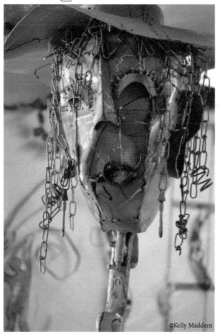

©Kelly Maddern

©Kelly Maddern

Once Abarn a Time

It's always a shame when an old, rustic barn has seen its final days. The beautiful, quality wood, aged by the weather and time, cannot be artificially reproduced. Repurposing the barnwood into beautiful, new, handcrafted furniture, home decor and rustic garden decor is what Once Abarn A Time has been doing since 1996. Located in Menomonie, this small company has been creating mirrors, frames, birdhouses, tables, chairs and much more since 1996. Many of the creations are accented with old rustic hardware and barn finds, including old nails, knobs, windows or other decorative pieces they come across

©Once Abarn a Time

Jill Chandler started Once Abarn a Time after she saw a photo of a barnwood table and knew she could do that. When she and her husband, Mike, moved back to Wisconsin from Texas, he started his own construction company and she continued to grow her barnwood repurposing company. Eventually Mike decided that he enjoyed woodworking more than his construction business and joined Jill in her venture.

The pieces of woodwork that Mike and Jill create are all one-of-a-kind. They don't have any favorites, they are just excited to come up with new ideas and see how an old barn window and screen

©Once Abarn a Time

transforms into a new flag or how a doorknob becomes an embellishment on a picture frame. They take a lot of custom requests and encourage the orders. In the future, they would love to do more custom work for artists and photographers and less of the art and craft shows.

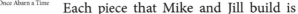

Mike and Jill do not purchase the wood they use. They take scraps from old barns that they find on Craigslist, at the dump or from farms they come across on the side of the road. The Chandlers once sought leads on places to acquire barnwood, nails, windows and doors – they now have to turn away offers because they receive so many. Barn donors are usually repaid with a custom piece that the Chandlers build for them.

Each piece that Mike and Jill build is time consuming. With the amount of time it takes to find and collect the wood, haul it, clean it up, design, measure and cut, a lot of hours have been spent on the piece before they can even begin to build it. The wood that they work with is far from perfect, so the Chandlers use their creative and artistic touch to see the wood into the new creation.

Word-of-mouth has allowed the business to grow in a way that allows Mike and Jill to control their operation. With the help of Etsy, Pinterest and Facebook, Jill

©Once Abarn a Time

is able to connect with people from all over the country and show off their products. The galleries of product photos around the web also help customers dream up their own custom orders.

If you want to learn more about Once Abarn a Time or place your own custom order, here are several ways to connect with Mike and Jill Chandler:

Website: www.onceabarn.com

Etsy: www.etsy.com/shop/onceabarnatime

Facebook: www.facebook.com/pages/Once-Abarn-A-Time/372062396372

Pinterest: www.pinterest.com/onceabarnatime/

Email: onceabarn@hotmail.com

Phone: 715 556-4491

©Kelly Maddern

NORTHWOODS WISCONSIN

The Northwoods are very unique compared to the rest of Wisconsin... and much of the Midwest. The combination of forests, hundreds of lakes and Lake Superior make this a year-round destination spot. Whether you are someone who likes to get out and enjoy the outdoors or you prefer to take in the sights and sample some wine, there are plenty of activities for you to enjoy in northern Wisconsin.

A trip to the Northwoods will remove you from the big cities and get you away from where most cell phones work. It very different from southern Wisconsin, as there are numerous dirt roads with ATV and snowmobile routes. Cars and trucks are not necessarily the most popular means of transportation. Depending on the season, boats, horses, ATVs, and snowmobiles may be the preferred means of travel.

If you visit the Northwoods seeking restaurants, shopping, wineries, resorts and gambling, you will be pleased. But just a warning, don't attempt to see and do everything in one visit. You will need many trips to experience all the Northwoods has to offer.

In Bayfield County alone, there are over 180 miles of trails for off-road vehicles. The trails are in addition to the roads marked for ATV use, which include city streets. Non-residents are required to purchase a trail pass. Riding off the marked trails is not allowed. Obtain a trail map before heading out, which includes rules and guidelines for safety.

Bayfield, a popular resort town along Lake Superior, is the gateway to the Apostle Islands. The town, home to about 530 residents, is a destination spot for fishing, boating and shopping. Every October, Bayfield's Apple Fest brings around 40,000 people to town. Known as the berry capital of Wisconsin, Bayfield is well-known for the many local orchards that benefit from the cool, moist climate.

Fish boils are a summertime tradition in Scandanavian communities along the coasts of the Great Lakes. Typically, white fish is boiled, with an audience, around an outdoor fire. When the fish oils rise to the top of the pot, kerosene is added to the fire to create a boilover, and the fish is done.

Lake Superior's sandy beaches along the Wisconsin coast are a great place for swimming, picnicking or just relaxing. If you get out to Madeline Island, the largest of the Apostle Islands, there is a beautiful beach at Big Bay State Park. If you are exploring the mainland, there are beaches to explore all along the northern edge of the state. Meyers Beach, near Cornucopia on the western side of the Bayfield Peninsula, is a popular spot for kayakers to depart from to explore the sea caves. The caves can also be reached by taking the nearly two mile long Lakeshore Trail.

While out sight-seeing, you will come across numerous shops in small towns. This shop with bluffs in the background was found in Nelson, along the Great River Road (Highway 35). The Great River Road runs parallel to the Mississippi River, through 33 cities, along 250 miles of road, from Kieler in the southern corner of the state, up to Prescott, where the river meets with the St. Croix River and takes a turn into Minnesota.

Interstate State Park, Wisconsin's oldest state park, was established in 1900. Across the St. Croix River from the Wisconsin side of the park is Minnesota's Interstate State Park. Above you can see what are called glacial "potholes" that are the deepest in the world. The park has several trails, a swimming beach and a campground. The park is very active year-round with activities such as kayaking, canoeing, biking, hiking, swimming, wildlife watching, cross country skiing, snowshoeing, rock climbing, and much more.

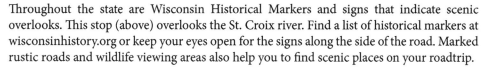

Throughout the state are Wisconsin Historical Markers and signs that indicate scenic overlooks. This stop (above) overlooks the St. Croix river. Find a list of historical markers at wisconsinhistory.org or keep your eyes open for the signs along the side of the road. Marked rustic roads and wildlife viewing areas also help you to find scenic places on your roadtrip.

Public boat launches are located all along Lake Superior. Along the Apostle Island National Lakeshore, rules for boating and personal watercraft may be different than other public waters. Be sure to review the boater's guide before heading out.

The Apostle Islands are made up of 22 islands in Lake Superior, north of Bayfield. The scenic islands are popular for camping, hiking and kayaking. The sea caves on the Apostle Islands are some of the best in the Great Lakes, specifically the North Shore of Devil's Island, Squaw Bay on the west side of the Bayfield Peninsula and Swallow Point on Sand Island. It is important to remember that kayaking in Lake Superior is much different than the other lakes and rivers of Wisconsin. The weather and water conditions just off of the mainland may be much different from what you will experience out by Devil's Island. You should get a weather report before you head out. It is also important to kayak with others. Lake Superior is very cold and your attire should be considered in case you fall out of your boat. Based on the 1-10-1 Principal, after you have fallen out of your boat, you have one minute to gain control of your breathing, 10 minutes to get back in the boat before you lose control of your hands, arms and legs, and one hour before you lose consciousness and become hypothermic.

Willow River State Park is located near Hudson and one of the most visited state parks in Wisconsin. The park includes: a beach along Little Falls Lake that is great for swimming and boating, around a dozen hiking trails, trout fishing along the Willow River and camping with several different sections of campsites. Willow Falls Trail is a nearly mile long trail from the campgrounds to Willow Falls that follows the shoreline. As you get close to Willow Falls, you can hear the rush of the water. The cascading waterfall is wide and beautiful. Over the falls is a bridge with a great view up and down the river. Across the bridge from the trail is a tower of stairs to bring you up and over the falls. People rock climb along the walls of the river and others wade in the waters and behind the main drop.

Grandad Bluff is located in LaCrosse and is the largest bluff in the area. This scenic overlook can be seen from most points in the city. The park features bluffside trails and a shelter with tables and fireplaces. The perfect spot for a wedding or family reunion. Parking and restrooms are available in the park. New Year's fireworks are launched from Grandad Bluff for the whole city to see.

Bluffs are common along the western edge of the state, along the Mississippi, Wisconsin and St. Croix Rivers. The landscape remains virtually unchanged from thousands of years ago, when much of the rest of the state was plowed over by the glaciers that pushed through. Perrot State Park in Trempealeau is a beautiful area of the state with gorgeous bluffs, like in the photo below.

Driftwood washed up on the beaches of Lake Superior is used to make art pieces, furniture and decoration in fish tanks.

Highway 13 (pictured right) guides you to some of the northern-most points in the state. This beautiful stretch of road was found along the western side of the Bayfield peninsula.

Wisconsin Point, in Superior, along with the connecting Minnesota Point, make up the largest freshwater sandbar in the world. Ten miles long, to be exact. Wisconsin Point is a popular stop for all sorts of birds during their Spring and Fall migrations. The Wisconsin Point Lighthouse was built in 1913 and visitors can walk the rock pier to reach the lighthouse. This lighthouse sits at the entrance to the Superior Harbor. According to boatnerd.com, the vessel pictured below is American Victory. The ship was launched in 1942 and was hit by a bomb from a Japanese plane while refueling a destroyer in 1944. She is 730 feet in length and can carry up to 26,300 tons of cargo.

The Northwoods get their name from the vast amount of forests that cover the land. Several national forests and other county forests help to make up the half-million acres of public forest available for recreation. The Northwoods also has over 3200 lakes and rivers to play in. For anyone looking to enjoy the outdoors, the Northwoods is the perfect place to spend your time year-round. According to friendsofthebrule.com, Wisconsin's 15.7 million acres of forest land break down in ownership like this: Private/Individual 57%, National Forest 9%, State 5%, Forest Industry 7%, Tribal Lands 2%, County & Municipal 15%, Private Corporation 4%, and other Federal 1%.

Wisconsin is home to 15,000 lakes. This number is disputed and different from source to source. This statistic likely includes bodies of water that are less than 10 acres. Eagle River is said to have the largest concentration of freshwater lakes in the world with their chain of 28 lakes and over 174 miles of shoreline.

Wisconsinlakes.com is a great resource for learning about the lakes throughout the state. The website includes information about the closest town, the lake size and lake notes, such as depth and types of fish that can be found in the lake.

On the same website you can also find other Wisconsin references for golfing, camping and more.

Along the bluffs in Fountain City, overlooking the Mississippi River, you can find Hawk's View Cottages and Lodges. The five cottages are built into the side of the steep, wooded bluffs and are a beautiful place to stay for your north woods vacation. You can find more information at hawksview.net about their rates and cottages. They also have a vineyard along highway 35, overlooking the Mississippi. In downtown Fountain City, you can stop in to their tasting room, wine shop and wine bar, located in an 1870s vintage building just off of highway 35.

Amnicon Falls State Park is located in Douglas County, not far from Superior.

The park features trails, a covered bridge, beautiful waterfalls and rapids. The covered foot bridge provides a great view of the river and the falls, while leading you through the trails.

This park is a great place for camping, hiking and enjoying nature. Keep an eye out for all sorts of animals, inland and along the river. Early morning is the perfect time to listen and watch for birds.

Binoculars and bird guides are available to borrow at the park office.

Copper Falls State Park (above) is located northeast of Mellen, in Ashland County. The Copper Falls, named for the color of the water and the history of copper mining in the area, is the first drop along the Bad River.

Many, many years ago, lava flows and glaciers worked their way through the area to create the beautiful gorges and waterfalls that exist today. As one of the most beautiful places in the state, this state park is a popular place for recreation. Besides walking the trails through the park, there is swimming, biking, picnicking, picture taking, bird/animal watching, fishing and camping to be done.

Allow yourself the time to enjoy!

Pattison State Park is located just south of Superior and is home to Big Manitou Falls (above) and Little Manitou Falls along the Black River. Big Manitou falls is the highest waterfall in Wisconsin at a height of 165 feet. Camping, swimming, hiking and picnicking are just some of the activities you can take in on the park grounds. In the winter, the park is open for skiing along several miles of beginner to moderate trails. A few trails are also available for showshoeing. The beach at Interfalls Lake is a beautiful, 300 foot stretch of sand. The lake reaches depths of 7 feet to 13 feet after a rain.

If you head three miles west of New London on Highway 54, you will come upon this old farm equipment that has been formed into the "Mukwa Motel." The motel's "concierge", a retired farmer named John Kraske, began developing this roadside attraction over 20 years ago. It is clear he has quite the sense of humor. His message seems a little less clear, but it's funny regardless. It was an interesting roadside find.

Along the Wolf River, raft fishing is popular during the spring walleye run. The custom-built rafts require a $5 permit and an additional $20 for inspection. Each raft is required to have an outhouse, fire extinguisher, smoke detector, carbon monoxide detector and life jackets. During the walleye run, families may go about their normal work and school routines and then meet back at the raft each evening for dinner, fishing and to sleep. Others schedule vacation during this time and spend an entire week on the raft.

Round barns and covered bridges are a fun find when you are out sight-seeing. Dale J. Travis has a website that documents round barns and bridges throughout many of the states in the US. This one I found outside of New London (pictured left) is included on his website: dalejtravis.com.

©Kelly Maddern

SOUTHWEST WISCONSIN

The Southwest corner of Wisconsin, the Driftless Region, was left untouched by the bulldozing glaciers that plowed through the rest of the state. The hills and valleys are rugged closer to the Mississippi River and the further away from the river you get, the terrain eases into gentle rolls. If you haven't spent any time here, it is highly recommended. Photos cannot do its beauty any justice.

The largest concentration of Amish settlements can be found in this area of the state, between Ontario (the canoe capital of Wisconsin) and Cashton. The Amish goods that they sell at farmers' markets or in their own shops are of the finest quality. They sell baked goods, furniture, quilts, baskets and more. Because they live simply and refuse modern conveniences, the products they make are not mass produced and are built with care. Cars need to share the road with their horse-drawn buggies, an uncommon sight through the rest of the state.

It is also in this driftless region that you can find the largest concentration of cold water streams in the world, including the Kickapoo River, which is the most crooked river in North America. Though the river is around 130 miles long, the distance from its beginning and end is only 65 miles.

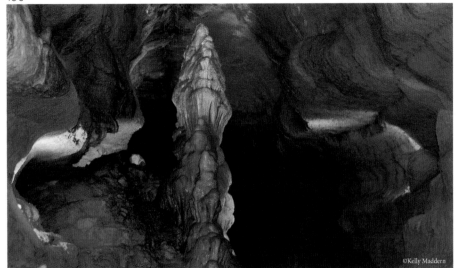

The Cave of the Mounds, a National Natural Landmark, is located in Blue Mounds. The cave is open for tours year-round, as the temperature always stays at 50 degrees. The cave began to form 1 to 2 million years ago and the features within the cave, such as the stalagmites, stalactites and columns continue to change. The growth of these formations are said to take 100 years per inch.

Having provided educational trips for over 60 years for schools, the Cave of the Mounds has been called "Wisconsin's Oldest Classroom."

The picture above is a view of a farm from the Infinity Room at the House on the Rock in Spring Green. This attraction, literally built on a tower of rocks, is world famous for the unique collections, largest indoor carousel and the original 14-room house. Alex Jordan, the original owner and builder, sold the attraction in 1988 to the current owner, Art Donaldson. Jordan passed away in 1989.

Wyalusing State Park (one of my personal favorite spots in the entire state) sits above the confluence of the Mississippi and Wisconsin Rivers. The views from the park are spectacular, and if you stay to camp, you can have these views right from your tent. The park has over 14 miles of trails of varying levels of difficulty. Sturdy shoes with traction are recommended for navigating the slippery stairways and climbing a ladder up to the Treasure Cave. The park also features a 6-mile canoe trail and two bike trails. Hunting, fishing, picnicking and play-grounds are also activities available in the park. Skiing, hiking and snowshoeing trails are available in the winter. Beautiful frozen waterfalls are a treat to find on your winter trek.

Husher Wayside Park, along Highway 131 in Crawford County, is nothing more than a place to drive through and get out to take in the scenery. But the scenery is spectacular from this high point overlooking valleys and other hills. Cows, trees, rivers, and farms dot the land as far as the eye can see.

Governor Dodge State Park, near Dodgeville, is one of the largest state parks in Wisconsin. With over 5300 acres, the park is great for hiking, biking, camping, boating, horse riding, winter skiing, ice fishing and much more. The park has more than 20 miles of bridle trails, as well as horse campsites. With the very steep and hilly terrain, sledding is a popular activity at the park in the winter. Snowmobiling is also allowed on the 15 miles of scenic trails within the park. The trail joins with the 40-mile Military Ridge trail for additional riding. Wildlife viewing is popular at Governor Dodge. Over 150 species of birds and many other types of animals have been observed within the park. For those looking to learn more about nature, the park offers naturalist programs throughout the year.

The Wisconsin River, known as the nation's hardest working river and the state's longest river, runs 25 hydroelectric plants along its 430 miles. The river begins in northern Wisconsin, close to the Michigan border and flows south through Wisconsin Dells and then turns westward as it reaches the southwest corner of the state. The Wisconsin River flows into the Mississippi River by Wyalusing State Park. Many types of fish can be found in the river, making it a popular fishing destination.

The unique and amazing sight that is the Dickeyville Grotto was built from 1925 to 1930. The grotto is made from materials that were collected from all over the world. Sea shells, glass, fossils, wood, rock, coral and pottery is a short list of some of the materials used. Several shrines are found on these grounds at the Holy Ghost Church. Besides the main shrine, the other shrines have their own themes such as the Stations of the Cross and a Patriotic display.

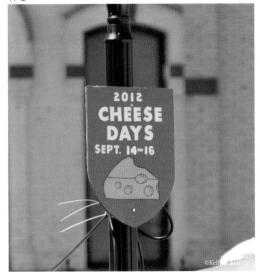

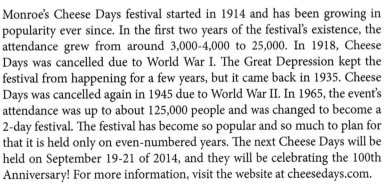

Monroe's Cheese Days festival started in 1914 and has been growing in popularity ever since. In the first two years of the festival's existence, the attendance grew from around 3,000-4,000 to 25,000. In 1918, Cheese Days was cancelled due to World War I. The Great Depression kept the festival from happening for a few years, but it came back in 1935. Cheese Days was cancelled again in 1945 due to World War II. In 1965, the event's attendance was up to about 125,000 people and was changed to become a 2-day festival. The festival has become so popular and so much to plan for that it is held only on even-numbered years. The next Cheese Days will be held on September 19-21 of 2014, and they will be celebrating the 100th Anniversary! For more information, visit the website at cheesedays.com.

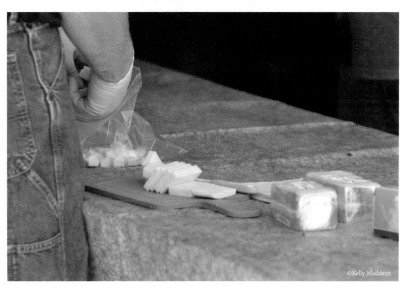

There are many activities to take part in during the weekend of Cheese Days. Besides the obvious – eating cheese – there are beer tents, cheese-making demonstrations, bands, dancers, kids' activities, a street dance, cow milking competitions, farmers' market, food tents, dairy farm tours, Green County barn quilt tours, a car show, cheese sandwich contest and so much more. Perhaps the most popular spot of the whole festival is the long line to get your hands on fresh cheese curds. It is said to be well worth the wait, which averages around 45 minutes. Green County is rich in Old World Swiss heritage, so part of the Cheese Days experience involves learning about Swiss traditions and foods.

Natural Bridge State Park is located Southwest of Baraboo and features the largest natural arch in the state. Below the arch is a rock shelter that was once used by Paleo-Indians. By studying artifacts found at the site, archeologists have discovered that the shelter may be "one of the oldest dated sites for human occupancy in north-eastern North America." Charred wood was dated back to 9000-8000 BC and other artifacts date back 6000-7000 years.

This park is not staffed, but is open year-round. Two trails through the park provide about 3.5 miles of hiking and signs along the trails are informative about medicinal uses of native plants. Restrooms and picnic tables are provided in the park.

Devil's Lake State Park, located near Baraboo, is a year-round park founded in 1911. A 360-acre lake is situated between 500-foot bluffs. The north shore and south shore offer 3300 feet of beautiful beach to enjoy. Devil's Lake is popular for a wide variety of activities at all times of the year. Hiking, biking, rock climbing, camping, picnicking, fishing, canoeing, kayaking, boating, hunting, swimming, scuba diving, skiing, hiking, snowshoeing, ice fishing, and sledding are just some of the activities you can enjoy in the park. The nature center, located within the park, provides educational information for both kids and adults. Most of Wisconsin State Parks have booklets filled with activities for kids to complete and earn Wisconsin Explorer patches.

©Kelly Maddern

SOUTHEAST WISCONSIN

Southeast Wisconsin is where the majority of the developed urban areas and the majority of the state's population are located. These urban areas aren't like you'll find around other big cities. Just outside of bigger cities like Milwaukee, Madison or Green Bay, you will find quiet and scenic roads to get lost in.

A variety of landscapes are found in this area of the state. The flat lands are great for farming and you will find many farms throughout the southeast corner of Wisconsin. Down the center of the southeast region, also known as the Eastern Ridges and Lowlands, is the Kettle Moraine State Forest. The kettles within the moraine create a very scenic area from Holy Hill down to Lapham Peak and over to Eagle and Whitewater.

When you take a roadtrip in this corner of the state, especially when you allow yourself to get lost, you will be surprised by what you come across down each road. From the steepest hills to the flattest fields, you get a little of everything here.

Southeast Wisconsin has a lot of character. That character comes from natural as well as man-made features. Painted silos, wildlife, lakes, horse ranches, winding roads and wind turbine farms, for example.

High Cliff State Park provides a view of Lake Winnebago, Appleton, Oshkosh, Neenah, Menasha and Kaukauna from the 40-foot observation tower. Nomadic Siouan Indians built effigy mounds 1500 years ago where the park grounds are now. The mounds included the shapes of a panther and a buffalo. The park is great for many activities: hiking, camping, biking, boating, swimming, horseback riding, fishing, hunting, skiing, snowshoeing and snowmobiling.

Waukesha is a bigger city with a lot of beautiful rural features around the city or just within the city limits. The Fox River Park is a county park in the southwest part of the city. The park, set along the Fox River, has paved trails for running, walking, biking and rollerblading.Unpaved trails through the woods are scenic and great for all levels of hiking. Along the river, you can fish or launch your canoe or kayak near the family picnic area. Shelters are available for rent for your event and there is a nature play area for kids, including a 32-foot slide.

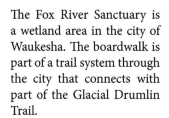

The Fox River Sanctuary is a wetland area in the city of Waukesha. The boardwalk is part of a trail system through the city that connects with part of the Glacial Drumlin Trail.

The Vernon Marsh, located between Waukesha and Mukwonago, is made up of 5000 acres of various types of land. The marsh is home to a large variety of animals and is perfect for hiking, hunting, bird watching, canoeing, trapping and fishing.

Holy Hill National Shrine of Mary is a church built on a glacial hill. The hill is 1300 feet high and located in the town of Hubertus. Holy Hill is the highest peak of the Kettle Moraine and sits on 40 acres of land. An additional 400 acres of surrounding land has been acquired to maintain the pensive atmosphere surrounding the grounds.

There are many things to do on the Holy Hill grounds. You can climb the observation tower for a beautiful view over the area. There is a cafe on the grounds that is open in the summer and many places to enjoy a picnic. The gift shop provides anything from religious to tourist items. Holy Hill is a beautiful place to enjoy the colorful fall scenery. It is a place where many people find peace, beauty and comfort away from their hectic lives.

Various wildlife areas can be found all over the state. The State of Wisconsin acquires land to be managed by the DNR which then provides a place for recreation for the public. The management of these lands allows the public a place to hunt, fish, hike, study natures and watch for wildlife. Some of the wildlife areas allow camping, biking, horse riding and winter activities.

A list of state wildlife and natural areas can be found at the Wisconsin DNR website: dnr.wi.gov.

THANK YOU TO THE individual CONTRIBUTORS THAT HELPED SUPPORT BADGER STATE OF MIND

Dan & Diane Maddern	Ryan O'Meara	Jean Kozak
Brooke Straks	Kellie Hare	Jennifer Smith
R.L.	Traci Meyer	Jennifer Anderson
Sue & Bill Wojahn	Allen Holzbauer	Dwight Reinhardt
Rusty Kapela	Tammy Buchholz	Peggy Sullivan & Rod Williams
Mary Toepel	Jean Kozak	Tabitha Dahms
Chris Parente de Costa	Stacey Tiggard	Karen Christensen
Lisa Church	Jaime Trevino	Jennie Ortega
Tonya, Erik, Edward & Helen Jacobson	Nixy Jose Morales	

I would also like to thank my wonderful husband, Jeff, and my kids, Kamryn and Cooper, for being so supportive and helpful throughout the work for this book. All summer we probably spent an average of 6 hours in the car each weekend day and during our week-long trips. They were troopers! Jeff also kept our house together, the laundry clean, and watched the kids during my hundreds of hours on the computer. I couldn't have done it without him. Besides making this book, we were lucky enough to have created a lot of memories while we traveled throughout the state. Thanks again - Love you!

Nenno — UNINCORPORATED		Neshkoro — POP 435		New Auburn — POP 551		New Berlin — POP 39,669	
Newburg — POP 1258		New Franken — UNINCORPORATED		New Glarus — POP 2174		New Holste — POP 326	
North Prairie — POP 2145		Norwalk — POP 643		Oak Creek — POP 34,626		Oakdale — POP 300	
Oconomowoc — POP 15,792		Oconto — POP 4490		Oconto Falls — POP 2876		Odanah — POP 1...	
Oregon — POP 9382		Orfordville — POP 1441		Osceola — POP 2557		Oshkosh — POP 66,344	
Osseo — POP 1711		Owen — POP 942		Oxford — POP 608		Packwauke — POP 261	
Petersburg — UNINCORPORATED		Petes Landing — UNINCORPORATED		Pewaukee — POP 13,224		Peyton — UNINCORPORATED	
Phelps — POP 1408		Phillips — POP 1461		Phipps — UNINCORPORATED		Phlox — UNINCORPORATED	
Pleasant Prairie — POP 19,822		Plover — POP 12,135		Plymouth — POP 8419		Port Washington — POP 11,272	
Port Wing — POP 406		Portage — POP 10,336		Princeton — POP 1216		Porterfield — POP 200	
Princeton — POP 1216		Pulaski — POP 3576		Racine — POP 78,853		Radisson — POP 242	
Randolph — POP 1812		Random Lake — POP 1589		Readfield — UNINCORPORATED		Readstown — POP 41	
Richfield — POP 11,342		Richland Center — POP 5182		Rio — POP 1062		Ripon — POP 7763	
River Falls — POP 14,889		Roberts — POP 1662		Rochester — POP 3682		Rock Spring — POP 36	
Sauk City — POP 3427		Saukville — POP 4459		Saxon — POP 336		Sayner — POP 584	
Seymour — POP 3472		Sharon — POP 1612		Shawano — POP 9263		Sheboygan — POP 49,13	
Siren — POP 809		Sister Bay — POP 877		Slinger — POP 5088		Sniderville — UNINCORPORATED	
Snows Corner — UNINCORPORATED		Sobieski Corners — UNINCORPORATED		Soldiers Grove — POP 595		Solon Spring — POP 59	
South Randolph — UNINCORPORATED		South Range — UNINCORPORATED		Sparta — POP 9602		Spaulding — UNINCORPORATED	
Speck Oaks — UNINCORPORATED		Spencer — POP 1930		Spirit — POP 292		Spirit Falls — UNINCORPORATED	
Spring Lake — POP 644		Spring Valley — POP 1352		Springbrook — POP 573		Springfield — POP 1029	
Springstead — UNINCORPORATED		Springville — POP 1140		Spruce — POP 947		St. Anna — UNINCORPORATED	
St. Mary's — UNINCORPORATED		St. Nazianz — POP 783		Stanberry — UNINCORPORATED		Stangelville — UNINCORPORATED	
Stanley — POP 3608		Stanton — POP 1278		Star Lake — UNINCORPORATED		Starks — POP 384	
Stitzer — UNINCORPORATED		Stockholm — POP 66		Stockton — POP 2904		Stoddard — POP 774	
Stone Bank — UNINCORPORATED		Stone Lake — POP 572		Stone — UNINCORPORATED		Stoughton — POP 12,6	
Sugar Creek — POP 3455		Sugar Grove — UNINCORPORATED		Sugar Island — UNINCORPORATED		Summit Center — POP 5232	
Summit Corners — UNINCORPORATED		Sumner — POP 952		Sun Prairie — POP 29,364		Sunflower — UNINCORPORATED	
Swan — UNINCORPORATED		Sweetheart City — UNINCORPORATED		Sylvan — POP 563		Sylvan Mounds — UNINCORPORATED	
Sylvania — UNINCORPORATED		Symco — UNINCORPORATED		Taegesville — UNINCORPORATED		Tamarack — UNINCORPORATED	
Thompson — UNINCORPORATED		Thornapple — POP 811		Thorp — POP 1621		Three Lakes — POP 2253	
Tibbets — UNINCORPORATED		Tiffany — POP 709		Tilden — POP 1356		Tilleda — UNINCORPORATED	
Topside — UNINCORPORATED		Torun — UNINCORPORATED		Towerville — UNINCORPORATED		Trade Lake — POP 852	
Trade River — UNINCORPORATED		Trego — POP 904		Trempealeau — POP 1538		Trenton — POP 482	
Tuleta Hills — UNINCORPORATED		Tunnelville — UNINCORPORATED		Turtle Lake — POP 1050		Tuscobia — UNINCORPORATED	
Twelve Corners — UNINCORPORATED		Twin Bluffs — UNINCORPORATED		Twin Grove — UNINCORPORATED		Twin Lakes — POP 598	
Union — POP 718		Union Church — UNINCORPORATED		Union Grove — POP 4915		Unity — POP 740	
Upper French Creek — UNINCORPORATED		Upson — UNINCORPORATED		Urne — UNINCORPORATED		Utica — POP 120	
Van Buskirk — UNINCORPORATED		Van Dyne — UNINCORPORATED		Vaudreuil — UNINCORPORATED		Veedum — UNINCORPORATED	
Veefkind — UNINCORPORATED		Vernon — POP 7518		Verona — POP 10,619		Victory Cent. — UNINCORPORATED	
Voltz Lake — UNINCORPORATED		Voree — UNINCORPORATED		Wabeno — POP 1219		Wagner — POP 749	
Waino — UNINCORPORATED		Waldwick — POP 524		Wales — POP 2549		Walhain — UNINCORPORATED	
Washington — POP 1919		Washington Island — POP 718		Waterbury — UNINCORPORATED		Waterford — POP 5368	
Waterloo — POP 3333		Watertown — POP 23,861		Waucousta — UNINCORPORATED		Waukesha — POP 70,7	
Waverly Beach — UNINCORPORATED		Waverly — UNINCORPORATED		Wayne — POP 2065		Wayside — UNINCORPORATED	
Webb Lake — POP 371		Weber — UNINCORPORATED		Webster — POP 653		Weirgor	
West Bloomfield — UNINCORPORATED		West Denmark — UNINCORPORATED		West Jacksonport — UNINCORPORATED		West Kraft — UNINCORPORATED	
West La Crosse — UNINCORPORATED		West Lima — UNINCORPORATED		West Middleton — UNINCORPORATED		West Prairi	
Weyauwega — POP 1900		Whitcomb — UNINCORPORATED		White City — UNINCORPORATED		White Corners — UNINCORPORATED	
White Creek — UNINCORPORATED		White Lake — POP 363		White Oak — UNINCORPORATED		White Pine Hav — UNINCORPORATED	
Wildwood — UNINCORPORATED		Willard — POP 605		Williams Bay — POP 2564		Wills — UNINCORPORATED	
Wilmoore Heights — UNINCORPORATED		Wilmot — UNINCORPORATED		Wilson — POP 532		Wilton — POP 5	

w Lisbon ...LATION 2558	New London POPULATION 7335	New Richmond POPULATION 8432	Niagara POPULATION 1621	North Freedom POPULATION 704	North Lake UNINCORPORATED	Northfield POPULATION 608	Northport UNINCORPORATED
densburg ...LATION 185	Ogema POPULATION 843	Okee UNINCORPORATED	Omro POPULATION 3531	Onalaska POPULATION 17,899	Oneida POPULATION 1144	Ontario POPULATION 557	Oostburg POPULATION 2879
Palmyra ...LATION 1786	Pardeeville POPULATION 2118	Park Falls POPULATION 2435	Pelican Lake UNINCORPORATED	Pembine POPULATION 1026	Pepin POPULATION 831	Perry POPULATION 856	Peshtigo POPULATION 3495
iacenza UNINCORPORATED	Pickerel UNINCORPORATED	Pickett UNINCORPORATED	Pierceville UNINCORPORATED	Pike Lake UNINCORPORATED	Plain POPULATION 778	Plainfield POPULATION 865	Platteville POPULATION 11,226
Potosi ...LATION 689	Poy Sippi POPULATION 1006	Poynette POPULATION 2532	Prairie du Chien POPULATION 5933	Prairie du Sac POPULATION 3997	Prentice POPULATION 652	Prescott POPULATION 4255	Presque Isle POPULATION 535
edgranite ...LATION 2153	Reedsburg POPULATION 9246	Reedsville POPULATION 1198	Reeseville POPULATION 707	Rhinelander POPULATION 7756	Rib Lake POPULATION 909	Rib Mountain POPULATION 5651	Rice Lake POPULATION 8441
Rome ...LATION 689	Rosendale POPULATION 1068	Rothschild POPULATION 5283	Rowleys Bay UNINCORPORATED	Roxbury POPULATION 1935	Rush Lake UNINCORPORATED	Salem UNINCORPORATED	Sarona UNINCORPORATED
boygan Falls ...LATION 7750	Shell Lake POPULATION 1348	Sherwood POPULATION 2741	Shiocton POPULATION 927	Shorewood POPULATION 13,228	Shullsburg POPULATION 1224	Silver Cliff POPULATION 535	Silver Lake POPULATION 2424
Somers ...LATION 9585	Somerset POPULATION 2653	Soperton UNINCORPORATED	S. Beaver Dam UNINCORPORATED	South Byron UNINCORPORATED	South Chase UNINCORPORATED	South Fork UNINCORPORATED	South Itasca UNINCORPORATED
lit Rock UNINCORPORATED	Spokeville UNINCORPORATED	Spooner POPULATION 2681	Sprague UNINCORPORATED	Spread Eagle UNINCORPORATED	Spring Bank Park UNINCORPORATED	Spring Green POPULATION 1637	Spring Grove POPULATION 1067
Croix Falls ...LATION 2133	St. Marie POPULATION 366	St. Francis POPULATION 9365	St. Germain POPULATION 1821	St. Joe UNINCORPORATED	St. John UNINCORPORATED	St. Joseph POPULATION 3882	St. Lawrence POPULATION 698
Stearns UNINCORPORATED	Stebbinsville UNINCORPORATED	Steinthal UNINCORPORATED	Stephensville UNINCORPORATED	Stevens Point POPULATION 26,717	Stevenstown UNINCORPORATED	Stiles POPULATION 1587	Stiles Junction UNINCORPORATED
tratford ...LATION 1578	Strawbridge UNINCORPORATED	Strickland POPULATION 300	Sturgeon Bay POPULATION 9144	Sturtevant POPULATION 6970	Suamico POPULATION 11,346	Sugar Bush UNINCORPORATED	Sugar Camp POPULATION 1809
unnyside UNINCORPORATED	Sunrise Bay UNINCORPORATED	Sunset Beach UNINCORPORATED	Sunset UNINCORPORATED	Superior POPULATION 27,244	Suring POPULATION 544	Sussex POPULATION 10,518	Sutherland UNINCORPORATED
Tarrant UNINCORPORATED	Taus UNINCORPORATED	Tavera UNINCORPORATED	Tell UNINCORPORATED	Theresa POPULATION 1262	Theresa Station UNINCORPORATED	Thiensville POPULATION 3235	Thiry Daems UNINCORPORATED
imberland UNINCORPORATED	Tioga UNINCORPORATED	Tipler UNINCORPORATED	Tisch Mills UNINCORPORATED	Token Creek UNINCORPORATED	Tomah POPULATION 9093	Tomahawk POPULATION 3397	Tonet UNINCORPORATED
Trevino UNINCORPORATED	Trevor POPULATION 6310	Trimbelle POPULATION 1635	Tripoli UNINCORPORATED	Trippville UNINCORPORATED	Troy POPULATION 2496	Troy Center UNINCORPORATED	Truman UNINCORPORATED
win Town UNINCORPORATED	Two Creeks POPULATION 543	Two Rivers POPULATION 11,712	Tyler Forks UNINCORPORATED	Tyran UNINCORPORATED	Ubet UNINCORPORATED	Ulao UNINCORPORATED	Underhill POPULATION 947
Utley UNINCORPORATED	Utowana Beach UNINCORPORATED	Valders POPULATION 962	Valley Junction UNINCORPORATED	Valley POPULATION 1352	Valmy UNINCORPORATED	Valton UNINCORPORATED	Van Buren UNINCORPORATED
tory Heights UNINCORPORATED	Victory UNINCORPORATED	Vignes UNINCORPORATED	Viking UNINCORPORATED	Vilas POPULATION 260	Vinnie Ha Ha UNINCORPORATED	Viola POPULATION 699	Viroqua POPULATION 4362
Walker UNINCORPORATED	Walsh UNINCORPORATED	Walworth POPULATION 2816	Wanderoos UNINCORPORATED	Warrens POPULATION 363	Warrentown UNINCORPORATED	Wascott POPULATION 800	Washburn POPULATION 572
Waunakee ...LATION 12,097	Waupaca POPULATION 6069	Waupun POPULATION 11,340	Wausau POPULATION 39,106	Wausaukee POPULATION 575	Wautoma POPULATION 2218	Wauwatosa POPULATION 46,396	Wauzeka POPULATION 711
lling Beach UNINCORPORATED	Wells POPULATION 582	Wentworth UNINCORPORATED	Wequiock UNINCORPORATED	West Allis POPULATION 60,411	West Almond UNINCORPORATED	West Bancroft UNINCORPORATED	West Bend POPULATION 31,078
st Richfield UNINCORPORATED	West Rosendale UNINCORPORATED	West Salem POPULATION 4799	West Sweden POPULATION 792	Westby POPULATION 2200	Westfield POPULATION 686	Weston POPULATION 633	Westport POPULATION 3778
hite River ...ULATION 889	Whitefish Bay POPULATION 14,110	Whitehall POPULATION 1558	Whitewater POPULATION 14,390	Wickware UNINCORPORATED	Wien POPULATION 795	Wilcox UNINCORPORATED	Wild Rose POPULATION 725
inchester ...ULATION 2006	Wind Point POPULATION 1723	Windsor POPULATION 3573	Winneconne POPULATION 2383	Winter POPULATION 313	Wisconsin Dells POPULATION 2678	Wisconsin Rapids POPULATION 18,367	Wittenberg POPULATION 1081

Made in the USA
Lexington, KY
21 January 2013